Master St. Elmo: The Autobiography Of A Celebrated Dog

Caro Senour

Printing Statement:

Due to the very old age and scarcity of this book,
many of the pages may be hard to read due to the
blurring of the original text, possible missing pages,
missing text, dark backgrounds and other issues
beyond our control.

Because this is such an important and rare work, we
believe it is best to reproduce this book regardless of
its original condition.

Thank you for your understanding.

MASTER ST. ELMO

The Autobiography of a Celebrated

Dog

A True Story
by
CARO SENOUR

Author and Composer of "Musical Poems" and "Flower Ballads"

Thirty-eight Original Illustrations

For Sale by
MILTON BRADLEY COMPANY
Springfield, Mass., U. S. A.

Master St. Elmo

My Mistress and I Home after a Walk

Dedicated to

BEAUTIFUL JIM KEY
The Most Wonderful Horse in
the World

ILLUSTRATIONS

INTRODUCTORY

To all lovers of animals, and especially of dogs, the "Autobiography of Master St. Elmo" will prove a delight. Many of the stories told of our four-footed friends are of homeless waifs, and our sympathies are enlisted because of their lowly estate.

Not so with the story of "Master St. Elmo," which is out of the ordinary—a life-tale of a dog of high degree, an aristocratic dog, to the purple born, as it were. No one who reads the true history of this celebrated dog can fail to become interested not only in St. Elmo, but in all other dumb creatures, for it reminds one that animals, like human beings, are susceptible to kind as well as to cruel treatment.

It is with pleasure that I introduce this book to the public.

Very cordially,

JOSEPHINE TURCK BAKER,
Editor "Correct English."

Through the kindness of Mrs. Augusta Evans Wilson, the Author of the splendid novel entitled "St. Elmo," and of her publishers, G. W. Dillingham Co., I have permission to use the title for my book "Master St. Elmo." The hero of my story having been named for the hero in the beautiful story of "St. Elmo."

CARO SENOUR.

MY MOTTO

By being kind to all animals, and by protecting Horses and
Dogs, you are befriending man's best and most faithful friends.

—ST. ELMO.

COPYRIGHTED 1904 · CARD SENOUR

How do You do, Little People? I am St. Elmo

MASTER ST. ELMO

CHAPTER I

OW do you do, little people? Permit me to introduce myself. I am St. Elmo, a tan-colored English greyhound, and I am six years old.

I have a wide, white collar around my neck, a white shirt-front, and white stockings to the knees. On my four feet I have white "Oxford ties"; my face is the color of my body, with a white part in the center of my forehead. My eyes are light brown, to match my hair. I am going to be very personal, and talk a great deal about myself, which is not always becoming, but I wish to impress upon your minds that even a dog can reason, and, therefore, I crave your forgiveness.

I am different from you, little friends, for I am *always* dressed. When I get up in the morning, I shake myself, and my coat and pantaloons are on, my hair is combed and face washed. I do not need a nurse-maid to dress me, but I seem to need one to tag me around, as I never *can* get away without some big person's calling me, or running along to watch where I go.

I suppose you know what an English greyhound is, but I do not; only one thing I feel sure about, it is not a very complimentary name, for I heard my master say one day, in reply to a question, that I was a "JOHNNY BULL"; then every one laughed.

Well, I will tell you how I happened to live in this big city, CHICAGO.

I was born way down in TEXAS, and when very young a

1

man took me away from my mother, brothers, and sisters, and brought me to a town in Kansas, called Topeka, where the wind blew so hard that I could not grow any hair; it all blew off; so that is why my hair is so short.   A few days

"Just Think! I was Worth as Much as Two Other Dogs"

after I landed in that very windy town, I was spied by a little boy named James, who told the man that he would give him two of his foxhounds for me (just think! I was worth as much as two other dogs).   My! I was glad to go to live with that little boy, for the man was cross and he did not know how to play with puppies, and I felt sure that the boy was taking me for his companion; so, soon we were the best of playfellows. I felt sorry for the other dogs that went to live with the cross man, who had taken me from my relatives (but then I've heard since that human beings sometimes give their babies away), so may be he was not so very bad. I was only three months old when I went to live with my

MY LITTLE MASTER "JAMES" AND HIS PET RABBIT

first little master. He kept me, in the day-time, in a yard with a wire netting around, and oh! how I wanted to get out and play in the other dogs' yards. *You* know, children, other yards and other steps seem so much better than your own, no matter how nice and large yours are. I used to poke my long, pointed nose through the holes in the wire fence when the other dogs passed, the dogs that had such good times seeing the town, and finding their own food and beds. At night I slept on straw in the barn, and wanted

my mother and brothers so much. Do you know that all
animals' hearts nearly break when they leave their loved
ones and their homes? That even the fierce lions mourn
when their babies are taken from them, and when they are
deprived of their freedom? I used to cry at night for my
mother.

At the end of a week my little master, James, brought
home another dog, and we soon became chums, and made
things lively about the place. His name was Klondyke—
they said he was a gold-mine. Of course I did not know
what they meant by that. He was white with one black
eye and a black tail. Folks said that he looked as if he had
fallen into a coal-bin when coal was twelve dollars a ton, because he did not match all over. Wasn't I glad to have a
bed-fellow? He was short and fat, and I was long and lean,
but we snuggled together and told each other our troubles,
and after a time we felt quite contented with our lot. I
rather envied Klondyke, for he was so small that he could
sneak out under the fence, and he used to see lots of sights
and had real scraps with other dogs. What a hero I thought
him when he told me about licking a dog bigger than himself. Sometimes I had to laugh when he came home with
the other eye blacked, or his leg bleeding. He had found
to his sorrow that he was not the only pugilist in Kansas.
I hope you will pardon me for using words like "licking,"
but my little master said these words, and he was all right
I thought, although he often got a whipping for saying such
words. My! how hungry I always was before mealtime.
I got the scraps left from the table after the big people's
dinner, and as there were three dogs, two cats, one cow,
a pony, two rabbits, and lots of chickens, sometimes
I did not get filled up. I then wished I was an only child.

The family had another dog, a dignified, well-bred fox-
terrier, and his name was "REX"—that means king. He
came before we did, so he felt his importance. He took

possession of the house, where we were not allowed, and
he, of course, got the best things to eat. I, being so thin,
there was a big place to fill in my stomach, consequently I
went to bed hungry many a night, and I don't know whether
even now I ever get filled up.

KLONDYKE

That was a pretty good home, but not the one I have
now, which I will tell you about later. My little master
showed partiality (something a parent never should do).
He would let Rex follow the pony, and oh! how much
Klondyke and I wanted to go. Sometimes Klondyke did
follow, and sometimes he came home in a hurry, too, yelp-
ing, and glad he was to cuddle down to me; that was when
his master had used the whip to drive him back. Don't

you think he was mean to us ? I tried to be very good, for I was frightened after the first and only whipping that I ever received. Klondyke seemed to forget how the whip felt, for he got lots of wallopings. I caught on from the first who was boss, so I made up my mind to be good, thinking to myself that when the gate was left open by mistake, and my master out of sight, I would run away and go back to my dear mother. I think little boys or girls who had been stolen from their mama would run home as soon as the chance came to do so. How should you like to be stolen from your mother ? Well! we doggies have feelings, too, and our poor mothers cry for us, just the same as would yours.

CHAPTER II

The time never came for me to make my escape, but a way opened for me to become an only pet, in the way of a visitor to the family. This visitor was my present mistress, who owns me (although I often hear her tell some one that I own her). When they take me out for a walk I hear them tell folks, "St. Elmo does not follow us, but we follow him." That is a mean thing to say, for a dog has to "rubber" around a little to enjoy himself, but my people want me to be a real dignified, well-bred canine, and walk in a straight line. Do you like to be so precise, boys?

I thought Topeka and that little back yard was the whole world when I was a puppy out there, and that Texas, where I was born, was another little back yard joined on (just as folks say in Chicago, that St. Louis is a suburb of Chicago). Wasn't that a joke, to think all of this big world was just Topeka? Every one makes some mistakes, and I never had studied geography nor traveled, so I want you to pardon me for not knowing better. Now I know that CHICAGO is all the world, and that all any one need know is, there is one great world, and that is Chicago. I feel very proud to be a citizen of this wonderful city (don't laugh, boys, I pay my taxes each year, just as all good citizens should do). At times it is a little uncomfortable for a dog, as well as for children, that is when the landlords will not take us in their flats, or hotels, or boarding-houses, or when the conductors will not let us ride in the cars, or the policemen let us play on the grass in the parks; then it is we have a hard time living, and we are greatly alike in our need of sympathy. Then that bugbear of dogs, the "DOG-CATCHER" (I want that name in the biggest type the printers have), keeps us in terror, and even

7

if we have a tag on and are loyal citizens these cruel men will
take us when they get a good chance, and then our masters
have to go to the "Dog Pound" and pay five dollars, five
great, big, silver wheels, to get us out—lots of poor unlucky
dogs are not taken out; then the men kill them with gas,
which is said just to put them to sleep and not hurt them;
and if this is so, it is a humane way to do. How I wish
every poor dog, horse, and in fact, every animal, could be
killed in that way instead of being shot, for animals do not
always die with the first shot, but suffer. I hope every one
will try not to make us animals suffer, for we are dumb and
can't tell our troubles as children can, and we are not respon-
sible for our being here. While I am on this subject, let
me tell you where there is a good home for stray dogs and
cats. That home is on N. Clark Street near Division Street,
and is under the supervision of the ladies and children of
the Anti-Cruelty Society. The Humane Society does lots of
good also, so there is no need of poor, starving animals on
our streets if each one will see that they are cared for.
Dogs do not go mad from kindness; it is from hardships
and abuse, and many a dog is killed for mad when he is
only dazed by hunger and cold. I beg of you, children, to
report all cases of cruelty that you see, and feed all hungry
dogs and cats, birds, and all other helpless animals in our big
cities. There is a nice little journal published in Springfield,
Ohio, called "Pets and Animals," which does a great deal to
help the cause. It is only fifty cents a year, and well worth
the price. Well, I was talking about flats and landlords when
I switched off on the humane subject, which is my mistress's
hobby. I can't say that I exactly blame landlords for refus-
ing to have cats in their houses, for they are really so musical
of nights that the other inhabitants can't sleep. They enjoy
perching on their neighbor's back fence in the wee hours of a
moonlight night and telling their love-songs in such long
drawn-out vibratory yowwwwwww-ouuuuuuuuuu's that even

a dog holds his ears shut. But then I like cats—most dogs do not. I would play with a cat if she would make friends with me, but she always sp———— at me, and puts up her back into such a hump, with her feathers all flying, that I get disgusted, and wonder if she knows how ugly she looks. That is the way I heard a lady say that her little boy and girl looked when they were cross and humped up their rose-bud lips; but, of course, I don't think any of my little readers do this, do you? I like to see cats run up a tree; so, sometimes when my mistress is not poking around, I chase them and stand under the tree and bark. I do this with squirrels, too, but I would not kill them, not even a rat. Why should I? I don't want to be killed, do I?

CHAPTER III

Now, I will tell you how I happened to move to Chicago. While I was in Topeka there came to visit at our house a lady and a gentleman. One day while walking in the garden, the lady spied me, at the same time that I spied her. Well! it was "love at first sight." I just ran to her, and she took me right up in her arms and squeezed me so hard that I felt my thin ribs squeak (she didn't mean to hurt me; was just loving me), and I was overjoyed at being petted. But I cannot yet forget a mean thing that she did say about me; when she put me down she said, "My! but he's all legs," and she also said, which I did not understand, that I was "A life boat on sticks." I have forgiven her, however, as I love her very dearly now. After that my life changed, and my living, too, for she wanted to fatten me up before she took me home. To my dismay, one day I heard her say, "We're going home to-morrow," and if you ever saw a dog's jaw drop and his ears droop and his tail fall between his legs, you have seen my picture at that minute. What was I to do? Poor me! I went over in a corner and wished again for my dear mother. That night I had dreams of cruel men, whips, and bones, all night. I ran to the lady (I did not know her name then), in the morning, when she came out in the garden, with my ears and head down and my eyes so bloodshot from crying that she knew in a minute that I was unhappy. She read my thoughts at once, for she said, "Should you like to go home with me, little dog?" (I had no name as yet.) I jumped up and licked her hand, and wagged my tail so hard that it nearly wagged off—then she knew that I had said "Yes." Turning to my little master James, she said, "Well, James, I will give you three dollars

10

for your yellow purp." Was not that complimentary to me?
How my heart thumped against my thin sides, for I knew
three dollars was an awful big lot of money. My little master
had only pennies to count and spend, so I thought it was a
joke, for how could I be worth three big silver dollars? I
decided that my days would be spent in the barn. But to
my surprise the lady took out three big silver wheels and
gave them to my little master, and took me up in her arms
for a second time and said, "Well, puppy, you belong to
me now, and I shall name you 'St. Elmo.'" You bet, I was
as happy as the boy who got his first pair of boots or pants
with pockets in. I could not thank my new mistress enough,
and I will tell you right here that I have never regretted
being sold to her. I did have a sorry feeling in my throat
when I said "good-by" to Klondyke, for I knew he would
miss me. I tried to tell the lady to buy him, too, but she
did not understand me this time — maybe she did know,
for I heard her say, "One dog is enough." A year later I
heard that Klondyke had another good home, and that he
could run and play outside the yard, so he was happy.
Poor Rex, the pet of the household, ate some poisoned meat
in an alley and died. He was a lovely fox-terrier, and the
family all cried when he died.

CHAPTER IV

The day after I was bought for three dollars, the folks went down town and brought back a bright collar and chain for me, and I was so tickled. That afternoon I went for my first walk, and when we got to the corner of the street such a big thing went whizzing by that my eyes almost popped out of my head. I was scared plumb through. When it stopped, the next thing I knew I was in this big, noisy monster, and was jerked from one side to the other until I wished I had not left my little, quiet home. Can you guess what this big monster was? I know, since I am educated. It was an electric street-car. Soon we got to the biggest house I had ever seen, with "Depot" in bright letters over the door; and pretty soon another monster, this time an Iron Horse, came puffing and snorting along, and stopped right in front of me. My! I was shaking all over. Didn't you get frightened, boys, the first time you saw red sparks fly up in the air and hot water blow out of the sides of this monster; and whistles and bells making such a noise that you were getting deaf? They call this frightful monster a loco-motive, big folks do. I thought how very nice it would be to be back in my cozy little barn, where such noises never reached us, and to snuggle down to Klondyke. You see, one is never satisfied, one always wants something different from what one has—it is just the same with man and beast. The worst was yet to come. My new master (he also seemed to belong to my mistress, so I guess she bought him for three dollars, too) took me into a big barn on wheels, where trunks and boxes were piled up, and he chained me to a hot-water coil (that is what the man said)—you see I know lots now, for I live in Chicago, where every one knows everything.

12

To my surprise, I was left in this big barn on wheels, with a strange man, who patted me on the head, and said he would look after me. He gave me a drink of water, and was very kind, so I made up my mind from that time to be good to everybody, and then everybody would be good to me. This has been my motto ever since, so this world is one big joke to me. The baggage-man made me a bed on some bags filled with hard papers, and once more I thought what a nice, soft bed Klondyke was snoozing on, the soft straw in the dear old barn. I spent most of the night thinking of my old home, and wondering where my new mistress had gone, as I could not see her, and I was hurrying along somewhere so rapidly that it almost took my breath away. Maybe, thought I, we are going back to get Klondyke. I hoped so, for that same big lump came up in my throat and almost choked me, when I thought I should never see him again. I tried to console myself by thinking that my new master was somewhere near, asleep on another hard bed like mine, in this noisy flying-machine; so, at last, from fatigue I fell asleep. All of a sudden a big whistle blew. How my heart jumped up into my mouth. Then the man packed more trunks up, and made such a noise that I thought what a lucky dog Klondyke was. I was the one now that wanted to cuddle down to him and tell my troubles. I did not howl, as some dogs do, as I felt sure the man wanted to be good to me, but did not know how, or he would not have blown the whistles. I got my reward for being good the next morning, when, to my joy, my mistress appeared, and spoke for the second time, my name, "St. Elmo." "Come to me!" she said. Well! walking was too slow; I just jumped and leaped to reach her, and I told her in as plain words as a dog can, how glad I was to see her and to be out again in the fresh air with my deliverer.

We stopped a day and a night in Lawrence, where the people met us at the depot with a carriage. I had never seen one of these trotting-machines, but I knew that when anything stopped in front of me now, I must get into it, so I was the first one in, not knowing how rude it was to be the first and leave the ladies to get in last. I am more polite now. I had been shoved into everything in front of me ever since I began traveling, so, of course, I got in, and took the whole seat, spreading out as much as possible for my comfort. How the folks laughed. My master, however, made me sit on the floor, and how I had to strain my long neck to see out of the window, for I did not want to miss anything.

We visited some pleasant friends in Lawrence, who gave me lots to eat, and let me play with their big dog, Punch. He was a brown water-spaniel, such a kind, smart dog. My mistress liked him very much, and so did I. My experience there is something I can never forget. It was planned for me to sleep that night in the basement with Punch, so the lady took me by the chain and started down a flight of stairs. I pulled back, for my! I was so scared when I looked down, because I had never seen a pair of stairs, and did not know how to get down. Did you, when you were three months old? I just stood still, and she nearly pulled my head off; still I held on, braced against the banister and the first landing. But soon my mistress thought of a way to help me, so she got in front and put first my right foot and then my left foot on the next step, and so on until I was down.

Is it not a funny feeling to go head-first down to nowhere? I believe even boys would be afraid to go downstairs head first. That night I had some good milk for supper, and a soft bed to sleep upon, and Punch for company, so I decided that I was progressing rapidly in the upper classes of society. What a relief it was not to hear those horrid noises. I slept so soundly that night that my mistress had to call me three times in the morning before I could get my eyes open. Then I had another lesson in stepology. This time the lady pulled again, and my mistress pushed from behind, causing

me to knock my thin knees against the sharp edges of the
steps, and to fall all the way up. Sometimes I was on my
knees, and part of the time on my feet, but they kept on
pulling until I was once more at the top, dizzy, but thankful
that the lesson was over. You see, I have always had a
school in my own house, with just one pupil (and that pupil
poor me), but three teachers; so I think I have had a harder
time than if my school had fifty pupils, for I am watched
every minute, and so much more is expected of me. After
that experience I decided that if there were any more steps to
climb, Master St. Elmo would climb them by himself, asking no assistance.

CHAPTER V

I told you in chapter four how I got home after this little visit in Lawrence, which is near Topeka, so I will continue my story from my arrival at the depot in Chicago, after that long ride on the "choo-choo" cars (that is what a little boy called them). We reached Chicago in the day-time, so I had a chance to see what a clean, smokeless, quiet, easy-going, unpretentious, exclusive, and wonderful city Chicago was; and indeed it is wonderful, if it is not entitled to all the adjectives stated above, but I never will go back on my home now, and I will lick any dog that will say a word about our great Chicago. I heard a big man say one day that the United States was in Chicago, so I know now all about it.

From the depot in Chicago on my way to my mistress's house, we had to ride on another of those barns on wheels, but when I started to get on, a big man of great importance, with brass buttons on his coat, said, "Dogs can't ride, madam, on these cars"; and my poor mistress felt so sorry, she said to him, "Oh, but my dog can, for I will pay his fare, and keep him on the platform." So at last he consented, and we had to stand up for about two miles. I did not care for myself, but I felt sorry for my mistress. The man said she could go in, but my mistress said she would not go where her dog could not go. But to think that I had cost a great big five cents again! I surely was becoming quite an expensive luxury.

We arrived at last at what was to be my future home, and I knew, by this time, that I had won the heart of the strange lady, and that I was to be hers always. I was puzzled once more in this house, for I had lived only on one floor before, and here was a house above with folks living in it,

16

and before I could get my senses together to figure out this
problem, I heard my mistress from above call, "Come up
to me, St. Elmo!" I was way down somewhere alone,
and she was way up nowhere, as I supposed, so with one
bound I started up those high, slippery (I did not know they
were like *that* then), ungrateful steps, forgetting my first
lesson in step-climbing, but finding another lesson they had
not taught me, the way to fall down stairs, so I rolled back
to the last step, for I could not get hold of the waxy steps.
I was not hurt, but my feelings were most cruelly injured.
I pretended, however, that I was abused and hurt, so in a
few minutes (it seemed an hour), the lady came to me, who I
know now by the name of mama, and she said, "Poor, little,
long-legged dog, are you hurt?" I put my head on her lap,
and felt that I had found a real mother. She helped me
up those horrid stairs, and said that she was sorry for me,
that she herself did not like slippery stairs; that she believed
in carpets, more for comfort, and not for style. She also
consoled me by telling me that *she* fell down those steps once,
and hurt her arm, and that she was *more* than four months
old. From that time I knew whom to go to when I was in
trouble. That night was the first experience I ever had in a
house. I slept on the floor in the hall by my master's door,
upon the softest bed I had ever known. Before I made that
desperate plunge upstairs, I had noticed a comfortable couch
in a room, and I thought to myself, that is *my* bed, for I shall
at once begin to usurp what I wish. At the first peep of day
I got up and shook myself and walked to the top of the stair-
way and looked down. Everything was so shiny. The
steps looked like glass, so I hesitated. What if my mistress
should look out of her door and catch me! Then I thought,
I can surely get down without assistance, so I put one trem-
bling foot down, just on the first step, when—somebody
pulled a string and those stairs seemed to close up, and the
next thing I knew I landed in a heap on the first landing be-

low, with such a bang that I woke the entire household, each one running to the head of the stairs and looking over the banisters at poor me. By that time I had collected my remaining thoughts together, so I could pose in a most dejected style, with my head down, my long tail between my legs, my ears drooped, and forming, as the people said, a sad and forlorn living picture. Oh! how I wished I had never spied that enticing couch; that soft bed upstairs on the floor was good enough for me right then. My mistress ran down, and, to my surprise, instead of whipping me as I had expected and deserved, she sat down and took me in her lap, and patted my poor, dazed head. My wounds healed rapidly, and I went back to bed, with her assistance, and never tried that again (while little). For some time after that awful downfall to my pride, I always turned my head sidewise when I passed that couch, so as not to see the horrid thing, for it made a dizzy feeling come over me. The bed at my master's door served for several months, until one night I discovered a door open and a room unoccupied. In the mean time I had noticed that all the family had high beds to sleep upon, with white coverlets, and I often rested my nose on them and knew they were nice and soft. I wondered if they were good enough for the family, why they wouldn't be just the thing for me, and save them making an extra bed up for me on the floor. So, one morning I quietly got up on that unoccupied bed, and found solid comfort at last—that is, for a dog. What a dandy sleep I was enjoying, when my master discovered me, and with one flat-handed, evenly balanced spank, I landed in a hurry on the floor. Did you ever get one like that, boys?

Oh, dear! what a sad fate, but what a soft bed. I found out later that this was my mistress's best guest-chamber, all dressed up in lace and stuff (that is not necessary for softness or sleep). It did seem that I was possessed to do everything that a dog should *not* do, but I always have watched

out for soft snaps, and I usually get them, for people everywhere are so good to me.   Of course, my own family have to
discipline me a little.   I often wonder if my little readers
ever need any such lessons.   When I grew larger and
stronger, I tried another scheme, for I was always looking
for comfort, and this time it worked.   As the first blush of
the rosy dawn peeped through the hall window, I crept
noiselessly down those same steps (not so slippery, for my
sharp nails had worn them off so I could get a grip now),
into the library, and there I would spend the rest of the
morning upon that couch which I had so dreaded in my
early childhood, but which now is "dreamland" for me.
I used to do this every morning, and for a time I was scolded,
but I persevered, and at last I conquered, and this finally
became my own bed; and now when we all go away for the
summer, my bed is shipped with us.   Soon after, they moved
it up into the front bedchamber, and bought a new leather
couch for the library.   I sleep in the family bedroom always,
and no one ever thinks of usurping my throne.   One evening I found my mistress resting on the couch, so I ran to the
closet door where my whip hung, and took the whip to
my master, and he got right up and whipped my mistress off,
just as they used to do with me.   How glad I was that she
was bad, too.   I never get any hard whippings, but I pre-
tend they hurt, and I yelp.   Our people do not believe in
whipping children or animals; they think it demoralizes
them.   My mistress stops all the cruel men that she sees
whipping horses, or abusing any animal, and reports them
to the Humane Society, and she hopes all people and children
will do likewise, for she loves children and animals best of
anything in the world.   I know, because she said so.

CHAPTER VI

The family had a nice back yard full of beautiful flowers when they brought me home, and I was delighted to play in that yard for several weeks. I had no companions as yet, and as I was left out there all day I made friends with the flowers. I amused myself by getting acquainted with the vines, the flowers, and the grass. I dug tunnels in the velvety lawn as large as my body, and I would get right down into them and be almost out of sight. Oh, what fun, boys! Once I had seven good-sized tunnels all in working order; that was *my* busy day, and when my master discovered them, it became *his* busy day, for he used his hands freely upon my poor body. He seemed to object to my spending so much time in improving his back yard, and he tried to reason with me; but I was a little thickheaded, and did not comprehend. Later on however, he understood me, and I mastered him, and preserved the lovely back yard for my own use all that fall. Until the next spring my master's dainty yard, the pride of his heart, became a wonderful yard of subways. What surprised me the most was, that after I had romped around for a day or so, the grass disappeared as by magic, and not a blade of grass could be seen. You know how you feel when you are very happy. Well, that was the way I felt as soon as I reached our lovely back yard. That December, when the flowers had died (the ones I had left by neglect), I felt a curious desire to see where they came from, so I dug way down into the ground and pulled up bulbs and roots, and spaded the garden up in fine shape. At this time my master decided to turn over the garden to me, so he quit. The one mean thing that I did do, and that I was ashamed of when I grew older, was, after I had cleared the yard of

20

bushes, bulbs, sticks growing up straight, and other unde-
sirable things, I discovered that I had left a vine clinging to
the side of the barn; and as I was doing a regular weeding-out

ADMIRING OUR LOVELY BACK YARD.

business, I ran up to it and put my strong teeth around the
tender stems, and then I ran as far out as I could, pulling it
all down and breaking it off at the roots. I *did* get a re-
minder for that piece of work in the shape of one, two, three,
four, the *four* being much harder than the rest. I was glad
then I had learned to count only up to four, or they might

have continued. *You* know what I mean; I can see you laugh at my expense.

The next spring when another vine was planted in the same place I looked at it with my eyes shut, when I had occasion to pass it; and as to the flowers and plants, I was willing to turn them and the entire garden over to the rightful owner.

As to the holes in the yard, I refused to dig any more, and I guess my master would have liked me to dig some for he used to take a spade and dig, dig, dig; but I never offered to help him. The grass failed to grow after that in our back yard, but the faithful flowers came back to please my master.

When I had to give up this source of pleasure, I got into all sorts of mischief. I enjoyed playing jokes on our cook, Miss Ellen, who really did love me. One day I had her scared; she thought that "Taffy" had been in her kitchen and had stolen a loaf of bread, for when she was in the other room, I had quietly taken her loaf of bread and was playing ball out in that very same back yard. That nice white bread I had soon molded into brown bread, in a much shorter time than it took her to make it white. My! but she was mad, and the family did without bread for dinner *that* day. I think now that that back yard sort of inspired me, for I did all kinds of mischievous things as soon as I made its acquaintance. Another day Ellen had set the table, and by this time I had grown tall enough to rest my nose on the table and see what the family were going to have for dinner. Upon this particular day I saw a shiny silver ball resting on a little silver stand, and I thought it would be such a giddy plaything, so I put my front feet up into the seat of the chair and helped myself. Do you think it is wrong to want things that you see? I spent a jolly five minutes tossing it up and catching it in my mouth, but soon I had my mouth full of tea. Just think! tea in my mouth. This I was told

afterwards was my mistress's pet tea-ball.   Well, you should
have seen the ball.   It was a flat ball when I had finished
with it, and it had to go to the doctor's and get fixed up
again; and now, when you put on your "specks," you can
find a wee hole where my tooth accidentally tunneled.   Of
course our guests do not know that I chewed it all up, so
they enjoy the tea just the same.

CHAPTER VII

I was very green when I first came to live on Calumet Avenue, and there was a little fox-terrier named Fritz, that thought he knew everything. He would not associate with the other dogs on the block, and was really very much "stuck up," so I could not but feel a little green when he showed so plainly his Chicago education to me. I was "hail fellow, well met" sort of chap, so up I ran to him the first time that I saw him; when, to my surprise, he made such a funny, bass sound from somewhere in his make-up, at the same time showing me his pearly, well-kept teeth, that I ran home for fear he might do as that big IRON HORSE did,— send forth sparks and smoke.

I wondered for many days whether that was the proper introduction for a society dog and a country dog. I had much to learn. After I had lived on *his* street for a month, and he had seen other fashionable dogs play with me, and people pet me (especially *his* master), he thought I was worth knowing. Then he tried to make up and get some of the attention; so he came waltzing up to me; but I stood firm, and said to him in as deep a bass voice as I could, "Boo!" and showed my big teeth; then I walked away with such dignity as only a well-bred animal can show, and he ran home to his "ma," and she shamed him and said, "That is what you deserved, Fritz, for being so discourteous to a new, unacquainted neighbor." I did not want to fight, although I knew I could whip lots of dogs, as I was so big and strong; but I also knew that it was not refined to quarrel or fight, for my master said so, and he never had a fight. After that, Fritz and I "never spoke as. we passed by," although each Christmas we exchange presents. He sent me a stuffed cat

24

last year with this tender greeting, "A merry Christmas, from your dear friend Fritz." I will say here that he is a very smart dog and very pretty, as you can see by the picture, and I have no hard feelings toward him now that we live fifteen miles apart, and I should like to have him come out and visit me, where dogs can breathe the air of freedom in good, peaceful Riverside. I must tell you of one present that Fritz sent me. It was a little white, curly-haired dog on rollers. I had never played with such dainty toys, so I just handled it as I did my bones. Pretty soon, while I was having so much fun tossing him up and romping hard, what did that naughty dog do but drop out two eyes, let fall his bell, tied with a pretty pink ribbon, and sprinkle his sawdust insides all over the parlor carpet. My! what should I do now? So I sat down with my poor dog be- tween my paws, and wondered

FRITZ

how I could get his insides in again and put in his eyes. While I was fussing with him, what did the un- grateful fellow do but drop his ear in front of my paw; that made me cross, and I went to work at once to get at the foundation of his anatomy, and so I pulled off each roller, took off his other ear, grabbed him by the tail and threw him across the room, when, horrors! his tail stayed in my mouth, but the dog had landed on my mistress's best bric-a-brac, and — BANG! I heard something go. Poor me! Had Santa Claus been good to St. Elmo? No! I wished I had not been presented with a Christmas gift, and especially a puzzle-put-me-together dog, for I could see no way to put him back as he was. I tried to look innocent when my master came in, but somehow my folks can always tell just by my looks when I have been in mischief; so he asked me what kind of battle had been going on here, then he picked up the poor doggie's eyes (which were two black shoe-buttons); then he found the ears, the tail came next, but where was the dog? No one could find the dog. I really hoped he had run back to Santa Claus to get repaired, but no such good luck. My mistress appeared, her sharp black eyes spied her broken treasure, and also poor, disabled doggie, that could not get away, and that broke the unnecessary article, which really was in the way, anyhow. I was talked to and reasoned with, but not whipped, as I heard them say that it was too cunning in him to whip him. I had a little trouble, though, getting the fuzz out of my mouth and teeth, for the dog was so covered with wool that I could not avoid getting some off.

I wonder if it hurt him, as it does me when they pull my tail? His nose didn't come off, so I think it was tacked on. My nose was full of sawdust and fuzz after the tussle, and I sneezed and sneezed and sneezed. If I am made of sawdust like that puzzle dog, I hope another bad dog will some time get his fill of sawdust, as I did.

The Sunday-school teaches us to forgive and forget; so I have forgiven Fritz, but I still have a lingering nightmare of his Christmas gift to me of an ungrateful woolly-dog.

CHAPTER VIII

One day during that winter, I went for a walk with my mistress on Thirty-first Street, and while passing along, I saw, to my terror, a big Indian standing right on the sidewalk a few feet from us, leaning against the front door of a store. My! I made one leap into the street, and I thought he was after me. He was all dressed up in leather, and blue, and red, and all colors, and had feathers on his head. I thought that if he killed poor birds to get his hat, that he might want me to make some tan leggings out of, for he held in his hand a bright glistening tomahawk. I thought surely he would kill my mistress, 'cause she stood right under him, calling to me. I wondered why she did not run. Maybe she was so frightened she could not run, so I decided to protect her, regardless of my own safety. I ran up a little nearer and gave one

THE WOODEN INDIAN

of my biggest bass-barks, but he did not move an inch; so I repeated it several times, each time more loudly and more emphatically, but still he gazed down upon us with that frightful hatchet ready to kill us. I did not know what to do next, but my mistress seemed so composed that I really thought she did not know a desperate red man from my master, for she was not one bit more frightened than when he is around. My senses came back with a shock when my mistress said in a loud voice, so that all the other dogs could hear, "What a goose you are, St. Elmo; that Indian is only a stick of wood; he is a wooden man, a cigar sign, put there to show naughty men and very naughty boys where they can buy tobacco, which undermines their health and makes their breath and clothes obnoxious." I was very much chagrined. Now I look twice at a man to make sure he is not wooden, before I bark and give any one a chance to call me names. What is a goose, boys? I always thought I was a dog.

CHAPTER IX

Hurrah for the Fourth of July! Hurrah! Hurrah! Hurrah! When Fourth of July came that year I was told that it was my birthday, that I was one year old, and that I was to begin school-days from that time; so my mistress said that I should bark once when people said "How old are you, little dog?" and that when people said, "How do you do?" for me to hold up my right paw and shake hands; something I never forget to do now, when people are polite to me. My mistress also read to me a poem which she wrote for the school children, and they spoke it on Mr. George Washington's birthday anniversary, February 22, 1898, and the paper printed it, so I guess it is all right. I will repeat it to you, with your kind permission (that is what big folks say, when they want to read something

HAROLD AND I CELEBRATING THE
GLORIOUS FOURTH OF JULY

that they wrote and that they think is good, but kind of want to apologize for reading). As Fourth of July is Mr. George Washington's day also, I think it is quite appropri-

29

ate to print it here, don't you ?   My mistress gave me quite
a talk upon patriotism, and explained all about the glorious
Fourth of July.

THE STARS AND STRIPES SHOULD WAVE
[By the courtesy of the " Chicago Daily Tribune."]

Some hundred years and twenty,
In the old colonial days,
A deed was done by one to save,
Who won our country's praise.
He was father, friend, and brother,
He was gallant, true, and brave;
And it is for him—George Washington—
The Stars and Stripes should wave.

There were many willing followers,
Who laid down plow and spade
To join their brave commander
In the cause to "Die or save."
They fought the fight which now to-day
Glad shouts of freedom ring,
And it is for these, our nation's brave,
The Stars and Stripes should wave.

We must not forget the later years
That brought us freedom, too,
And those who bore the same old flag
With Stars and Stripes anew;
They were also gallant soldiers,
Noble boys in faded blue,
And it is for these, our nation's brave,
The Stars and Stripes should wave.

With Stars and Stripes suspended,
Telling each their story old
Of the deeds of gallant soldiers,
Our loyal boys so bold,

We will ever praise and honor
  Those who fell; yes, but to save,
In the cause which makes us bow our head
  When we see "OLD GLORY" wave.

My mistress says that Fourth of July is not wholly in-
tended for play and noise, but that it is a day for thankfulness, for had it not been for the "Father of our Country,"
General George Washington, and his gallant soldiers, we
might yet have been ruled by the little strip of land across
the sea, not larger than one of our states. You all know
that the Declaration of Independence insures us the bless-
ings of liberty, and that the "Star Spangled Banner" waves
over every man, woman, and child in our beloved country,
protecting, and making us all better under its floating colors.
One of these beautiful flags hangs in our house always, and
whenever my mistress goes away she takes a small silk flag
with her, which was made for her, and hangs it in her
room wherever she stays. I wish every child would hang
a flag in the house that he lives in, for there is no
picture so grand, no statue so imposing, no decoration
so harmonious, as our honored and beloved flag with
the red, white, and blue—the red stripes as emblems
of our strength, the white for purity and love, the blue
the emblem of our trust and truth, and the stars the
emblem of protection, watching over us all, as the little stars
in the blue of the heaven watch o'er us each night. God's
flag is the blue of the heaven striped with the red of the sun-
sets, and His stars are the little bright eyes of His angels.
His mighty flag forever and forever waves o'er us, and we
feel sure of His protection; therefore, with such an emblem of
loyalty above us, we must feel the same protection on our
land with "Old Glory" waving over us.

CHAPTER X

On this most remarkable morning, my first birthday, we hung out our flags the first thing. After a while there began the loudest noises that I had ever heard (I thought that the big IRON HORSE was after me again). Most dogs, they tell me, run and hide when the Fourth of July comes around, but I was delighted as soon as I understood it was all play noise. I wanted to go right up to the big fire-crackers and see where the noise came from, but my master explained them to me, and said that should I go up to one and it was lighted, it would blow my head off; so, boys, you must be careful and not be too curious. I spent all the day watching and playing with the children; the louder the noise the better I enjoyed myself. I could not eat my breakfast, dinner, or supper—I had to stay right with the fun. The girls on our block had little round torpedoes to slam down on the sidewalk, but of course that was tame for the boys and me, so we fired off crackers. That night I was so tickled that I could not eat my supper; I was afraid I should miss something. I sat with my family on the front porch, watching the beautiful colored lights, and listening to the guns. The funny things that interested me most were the balloons soaring up into the air and the long-tailed fire-serpents sailing so gracefully against the blue sky, their little sparks matching the stars peeking through the heaven and dropping down in thousands, making even the stars wonder what these miniature starlets were which were adding so much beauty to their own far-away candled canopy of blue. I wonder what made them go so high and after a second disappear, just as though they had not been there at all. My! how things do puzzle me. I wonder if other little people

32

know the reason for such mysterious freaks of nature.   I no
sooner got through watching one big fiery snake shoot up
than a red or blue or green light would dazzle my eyes; then
a boom! boom! boom! and then another serpent, so my
neck was almost stretched out of repairable shape.   Still I
had the best time of my life, and thought it the funniest day I
had ever seen, and congratulated myself on having been born
on the glorious Fourth of July, so every one could enjoy himself celebrating my birthday.

CHAPTER XI

Soon after this I noticed that the trunks were being packed, so I knew something extra was going on. I stayed as close to them and to my mistress's heels as I could. I, of course, wanted to go also. We did go in August to a place called Minocqua, and this was my first summer outing. I know now that it is very stylish and swell to leave home in the summer, and quite the proper thing for fashionable dogs to be taken to summer resorts. As this was my first experience, I made many blunders and acted like a real country dog. The first thing I did when we landed at Minocqua was to make a bee-line for the first house that I saw, which happened to be a villa, and up I went and all through the house without introducing myself. After startling the whole family, I went into the next cottage and saw all that they had, arousing the children and causing great commotion, for I always rushed then instead of walking quietly. I was so excited that my people could not get me, for as soon as they visited one place, I had finished with that and was investigating another. I heard a little boy say to his mama, ''There is a little fawn out on our lawn, come and see!'' I soon realized what it meant to be called, or at least taken for, a fawn or a deer up in the wilds of Wisconsin; so I obeyed after my first lecture on hunters of deer, and Indians shooting deer, and stayed at home except when my folks took me into the woods with them. You see, I am the color of the deer in the summer time, and at a distance I could be shot for one if I were seen alone in the dense forests and brush. My mistress says that there is a fine exhibit of deer in the Field Columbian Museum in Jackson Park, in Chicago, showing them in all their different changes of coat and in each season. These

34

are of course dead deer, mounted, but they are perfect, and all children should see them if possible. The live deer are at Lincoln Park Zoo. This first day at Minocqua I had a scrap. There was another pet dog that was boss of all this place; her name was "Peggy," commonly called "Peg"; she was a brown water-spaniel and very much spoiled. She looked sidewise at me with a wild gaze, and I saw trouble brewing. As I was to be there three weeks, I decided to settle this little matter about possession at an early date, as soon as she wanted me to do so, and as politely as I could, seeing she was supposed to be a lady. I went down to the lake showing my independence and importance, and on the way back, I saw an old torn straw hat, such as the best fishermen wear to catch fish;

LIVE DEER AT LINCOLN PARK ZOO, CHICAGO

as it was not owned by any one apparently, and as I was rather bored at not having anything to do, I picked it up, and began to shake it, running up and down, passing the house where she lived, and enjoying myself immensely; when suddenly from around the corner of the house popped Miss Peggy; she took hold of one side of the brim, and I held to the other, she growling and saying, "You let go of this hat; it belongs to me." I said in reply, very politely, "Miss Peggy, I found this hat and it is mine, kindly let go." She still held on and pulled, when r-r-rip went the hat, but still we each held fast. Rip, rip went the old hat;

still we pulled, but this time the fair damsel parted from the hat with only a tiny bit of it in her dainty mouth as a souvenir. I dropped the hat and put my big foot down upon it with a firm hold, and looking at her with a most decided expression, I said, "I got this first." She understood, and after that we became great chums. She took me around the place, and even shared some bones with me. It is sometimes necessary to show the fair sex that we, the strong and heroic, have our rights also.

These people at "The Villa" had another pet, a most comical kind of a screeching pet. I guess she named herself, for she kept calling most of the time, "Poor Lauretta." She never seemed to me to be poor, for her cage was filled each day with fresh food and water. People called her a parrot. She was indeed very beautiful to look upon, her color being green with red on her head; she was all right if she had not wanted the first and the last word always; but she talked when no one was around, and when they came, she would keep on talking, and really I got awfully tired of hearing her say "Poor Lauretta," "Polly wants a cracker," when she was full of crackers. I never got very close to her cage as I was afraid she would snap at me, for she used to hump up her back and look just as cats do—and I have had my experience with cats—so I kept as far away from Lauretta as possible. How she used to fool us, that is "Peg" and me. We never did learn the difference between her voice and "Peg's" little master "Juny," for each one used to call "Here Peg, here Peg," and of course we both ran to the little master, when lots of times it was that naughty bird calling "Here Peg"; then she would laugh at us for being fooled. Even the big people could not tell which one was calling, as "Lauretta" really could mimic "Juny" to perfection. She had a fine soprano voice, and could sing in perfect tune and in plain words "Pretty, pretty Polly Hopkins, how do you do? How do you do?" If you children want to hear the tune, ask some dear old grandmother, and she no doubt can_sing it for you. There was something strange about "Lauretta" that made me afraid of her. She was too human, I guess, for I was not afraid of toads, frogs, snakes, bugs, chickens, or anything else, but *she* was a puzzle to me.

The country around Minocqua is beautiful, and such a picturesque lake! It has an awfully big Indian name, and you can find it on your maps marked Kewagasaga; it means, in Indian language, "little tomahawk."

After we had been here a few days, my master went out in a skiff on the lake, and he called to me. I went to the shore of the lake, but was afraid to follow him, for I had never been in a large body of water, nothing larger than the family bath-tub (and I never liked that). I don't like to be washed and have soap-suds rubbed into my eyes and ears, do you? Well! I just balked, so my master had to come after me, and to my delight he let me jump into his boat. Away we glided out, like a swan on the smooth waters, and I thought I had reached the height of my ambition, to see the world without footing it around. Misery! All I remember now is that I was pushed by some one (I have my opinion as to that some one), headlong overboard into the biggest bath-tub that I had ever been in. I could not touch the sides of it, so I thought I should die with fright. I splashed and I sputtered with my mouth filled with water, but at last I heard my mistress call from the shore, so I made one last attempt to reach her. I started to walk the same as I do on the land, but it would not do. Once more I heard encouraging words from the shore, this time from my mama, "Come to me, St. Elmo, swim, don't walk." In a moment I was swimming through the water in the easiest fashion, and finally I reached the shore, very wet, but very happy. My first swimming lesson was a sudden one but never to be forgotten, and now I dearly love to swim after the boat, and lots of times I am not wanted, then I laugh to myself, and think, I guess you are sorry you taught me to swim. If you boys have ever had such an experience in swimming, you will know how I felt, but if you never have been so treated, don't try it just because I told you.

After that I saw ''Peg'' and lots of the people go into the lake, even my mistress; so I soon enjoyed it, and would go way out after my inflated rubber ball. Later on my family had a hard time keeping me out of the water. I used to run up to them and shake myself so that the water would sprinkle all over and would rub my wet coat against them. Of course some did not enjoy the joke, especially when they were all togged up, but it was great fun for me. I pretended I did not know any better, so they would laugh and forgive me.

CHAPTER XII

The next object of my anxiety and suspicion was in the shape of a big red man, called an Indian. This time he was a real live Indian and did not carry a tomahawk; *he* always carried a bucket. When he came to the village, it was filled with berries, but when he left for home, it was full of "fire-water." He had a big reddish brown face and little black, bead eyes. He said his name was "Jack"; of course that was his English name. He lived eighteen miles from the village on a reservation called "Flambo"; that is also on your map, and if you do not know about a reservation, read it up, for a dog must not know more than a boy or a girl.

These Indians are of the "Chippewa" tribe, and they are partially civilized. Most of them live in wooden houses, still there are some old-fashioned Indians who hold to the wigwam and tepee. They do some work, at least the squaws (their comely wives do the work, and they spend the money). This big Indian Jack had a little boy pappoose who was carried on his mama's back when he came to the village; he was about my age. One day my mistress held out to him a lovely pink carnation (my mistress's favorite flower); this was in her left hand, in the right hand she held a nickel. The pappoose grasped the bright flower in his little fat brown hand, choosing the one he liked best, but papa Indian immediately took it from pappoose boy and gave it back to my mistress and made the little chap take the money. His papa had an eye to business just the same as the white papas have, and he was giving his son his first lesson in making money. The baby, however, went away with the flower, for my mistress loved the baby for loving the beautiful flower the best. The baby did not cry, and the Indian said, in reply to a question, "Injun babies no cry." The squaws make bead-work, baskets, mats, blankets, and belts, and many lovely things. I never got hold of any of these things to play with, although I often wished that I could have one of their bright blankets or mats to shake. You boys know how we dogs like to get things to shake and tear up.

I must tell you about a tiny pappoose whom my mistress saw at "Flambo." She was just three days old and as fair as any white child is at that age. She had a little white bonnet on, and was tied on a board, which was suspended from the top of the wigwam by ropes. She was tied there in the morning and not taken out until night; she never cried; you know "Jack" said "Injun babies no cry." The papa Indian said the pappoose was "no good," because it was a little girl. He wanted boys so as to make warriors of them. This and the thoughts of such a happy baby life, free from care, amused my mistress so much, that she wrote a song, the words of which I am going to give you here.

ROCK-A-BYÉ, LITTLE PAPPOOSE LADY

(Words to a Chippewa Pappoose)

Rock-a-*byé*, Little Pappoose Lady!
Daddy Injun's gone away, gone a-daydy;
   Went to hunt a red deer skin
   Just to dress his baby in—
Rock-a-*byé*, Little Pappoose Lady!

Do you *cry*, Little Pappoose Lady,
When you're hung up on a tree in the shady—
   And the Injuns, they all go,
   And you're tied from head to toe—
Do you cry, Little Pappoose Lady?

Where's your *doll*, Little Pappoose Lady ?
Oh, I see! on a bough for its cradly,
   'Tis a stick dressed up, that's all,
    With a blanket for a shawl—
But you're happy Little Pappoose Lady !

Rock-a-*byé*, Little Pappoose Lady !
Soon you'll journey with your tribe, far, to trady,
   In your carriage, on squaw's back,
    You're the happiest little black
In your freedom, Little Pappoose Lady !

Look-a-*heré*, Little Pappoose Lady !
Would you change and be a white girl baby ?
   Washed and dressed five times a day,
    Dressed in frills and ribbons gay—
Would *you* change, Little Pappoose Lady ?

    For those who do not understand baby-talk, "daydy" is "gone away";
"shady" is "shade"; "cradly" is cradle"; and "trady" means "trade."

    We next stopped at a place called "Eagle Lake," because
it is in the shape of an eagle with its wings spread. There was
a farm here where I liked to roam about for they had such
funny animals. There was a big rooster who raised nine
little turkeys; their mother had died, so master rooster
adopted the orphans, and after a time they grew so large
that when they perched upon the fence, four on one side and
five on the other side of father rooster, he looked so small
that you hardly noticed him at all. We left this lake and
went to Racine and there we got into a big boat; in my
earlier days I should have called this big sea-bird a barn on
the water, for you know all places were barns to me. I was
taken down into the basement of this big boat and chained
to a chair (just think, boys, of chaining a big strong dog to a
chair); this place was what they call the baggageman's

room.   Well, this man after a little went out, and I had had
my eye on his bed, so as soon as the door closed after him I
got up, pulled chain and chair, and got into his lower berth.
This was another soft bed, so I fell asleep.   I guess my
snoring out my contentment made the man return, for soon
I heard him crawling into the upper berth; so we both slept
the rest of the journey.   When my mistress came to get me
at the end of our trip, she was surprised at my audacity and
to see me in the better berth and the man way up on the top
bed.   She said, ''Do you know my dog is in your bed?''
''Yes, madam, and if your dog is smart enough to pick out
the softer bed, I think he is entitled to it.''   I guess I was
born a lucky dog.

CHAPTER XIII

Nothing happened to narrate until Christmas that year.
I should rather leave this out, but my story would be incomplete. We had spent a very pleasant day, had received
many lovely gifts, and had had plenty of good things to eat.
That always pleases me the most for I like good eating,
especially ice-cream and candy, and some kinds of cake.
Oh, yes! I forgot! I like English walnuts about the best.
After tea I was left alone for the evening, the family being
invited to a Christmas-tree party. Why I was not invited
I never could understand, as I played with the children who
had the party, and they appeared to love me very much. I
was really very sad at heart; why do you suppose they did
not invite me? Do you ever get left out of parties? Well!
it got rather monotonous after ten o'clock, so I looked all
around the floors and tables for something to play with. I
wanted to be amused, but I could find nothing to interest
me. After a little while I spied a paper box upon the library
desk, which looked as if it were lonely, too. It was so near
the edge of the desk that I expected it would fall off anyway, so I just put my front feet up in the chair and pulled
off this nice little alluring box. I was doubly pleased when
I threw it up and it came down in two pieces, for I then had
two boxes. What fun for a dog! I was glad I had stayed
at home; so I threw one of the two boxes up again and once
more I had an extra box, *this* time three. The third box I
found had something in, so up I sent it, higher than any of
the others; when to my joy, a fourth box dropped at my feet.
Was I a magician? thought I, for I had seen my little playmate do such wonderful tricks. Yes! I was more wonderful than he, for I had materialized a most beautiful

43

picture, such as you see on the next page entitled "Little Boy Blue." It was a piece of glass, with this picture painted on it in pretty colors. I found out later that it was a lantern slide, and that it cost my master $1.50 and many days of waiting to get it home. It was so bright and pretty that I, of course, made a jump for it, and my clumsy paw landed right in the center and crushed the little glass all to pieces. I was so sorry, but how was I to know it was not to play with? So I started to pick up the pieces, but owwww! I cried, for they stuck in my mouth and a piece stuck in the side of my gums and I could not get it out. I lay down on the floor and my play was all over for that day. I knew that when my master returned and saw the damage I had done another place would sting. When they came home, I did not run to meet them as I was in the habit of doing, so they knew something was wrong—I always betray myself somehow. Presently my master discovered the havoc I had caused, and I got my little reminder as I had expected. I never am disappointed that way, are you? My master said, "You bad dog, you have destroyed a $1.50 lantern slide." Just to think I was suffering all the time with that glass in my jaw, but no one seemed to care. After they had picked up the four boxes, which I had made out of one, and all the glass, my mistress, who is always sorry when I am in trouble, came and asked me what made me wiggle my mouth, and she put her finger inside and pulled out a piece of glass a half-inch long, then she washed my mouth and said that I had been punished enough. After this I always waited for the folks to open their own packages. I was only one year and five months old when this happened, and I did not know any better. Were you ever left alone when you were as little as I was at that time? I am sure you think that I should have been forgiven.

My best friends are children. They can pull my tail, or ears, or poke their fingers in my eyes, and it is all fun to

Little Boy Blue

me whatever children do. I was very good after this mistake of mine until we went to Channel Lake in May. It seems as if I am always possessed when I go away until I get a dressing down. What makes dogs so full of mischief? I was very happy when we got to Channel Lake, for there was another big bath-tub, plenty of ground room, and lots of horses, cows, chickens, and pigs to bark at. I like to tease pigs, they grunt and make such ugly faces that it makes me laugh. The cows with the big horns I was afraid of, so I stayed behind the fence and barked at them. I am like a little boy of six, whose name is Paul, who said that *he* was only afraid of "loose cows." Wasn't that cunning?

There was the "Bog" to get into, and that was great sport. I spent many happy moments in the bog, hunting for frogs and scaring them out of their homes and jumping after them. I would not hurt them, only I enjoy the sport of hunting. I got their little hop, skip, and jump down pat before I left for my quiet home in the city. I had many scoldings for haunting this most fascinating place, for I always went home with muddy feet, and sometimes with mud up to my neck. I first became acquainted with this bog by watching my master over there looking for something, and he would come back with a bucket full of frogs, catching them in a net and using them for baiting his hook to catch another poor creature, the fish. Poor little froggies! *I* never hurt them. I was curious to find out where my master got the frogs, so after he returned I strolled over to the same place, and it soon became my favorite amusement. I wondered when my master came home with his feet muddy that my mistress did not scold him. She saw only *my* mud, so I got the lectures for the two. I think she was partial to him sometimes.

I must tell you about "Duce." He was a little puppy, white with two black spots on his side, so this is why they called him "Duce," that means two. After my mistress saw him, he was her dog, as all dogs are. She seems to have their love after a first meeting, so she renamed him "Two Spots," which name every one soon called him, and he seemed to like a two-syllable name better. He was a foot long and about a foot wide, and so fat he could hardly walk. He would start away on a run, but before long you would see him rolling the rest of the way. It did not seem to matter whether he toddled on his feet, back, or fat sides; he always got to the place he started for just as well as I did with my long legs. He had a pet name, "Butter-ball." His relationship was through a little girl whose papa owned the hotel where we were boarding. She was a darling little fair-haired girl, named "Marie." She was my dearest friend out there and my constant playfellow. We used to play until we were all tired out, then I would lie down under the shade-trees, and she would lie down with her head on my shoulder, making a pillow of me. This little girl was four years old. She was chubby like "Two Spots," and her eyes were blue. I used to love to have her dear little chubby hands pat my head. One day I saw a horse in a pasture, seemingly alone, and not having any fun, so I started after him, and when he saw me he "took to his heels," so off I went after him. We were having such fun when the family (there were so many in my family, three, that some one was always in the way, watching me) spied me, and I was called to account for chasing a horse. My mistress gave me a hard spank, with her hand, and I pretended that I was hurt so as to get sympathy, which I did get, for Marie had seen the abuse and had come to me, putting her chubby arms around my neck and telling me not to cry. My feelings were always hurt more than the hurt itself. "Two Spots" slept under the porch steps by our rooms, and he barked at every one passing, with the exception of our family, who could run down the steps all hours of the night, and he would come out to see them, but never bark, he knew their footsteps. He really thought that we belonged to him. The family to whom he belonged he barked at when they came down our steps at night. He seemed to think that he was really protecting us, and he wasn't much larger than my head, either. In the daytime he would watch under my mistress's hammock and not allow any one to go near her wihle she slept. He seemed to think he was her protector. It made me a little jealous, for he was small, and he often got into the hammock and slept with my mistress, while "poor me" had to lie on the ground. That is what one gets for growing so fast. I liked sleeping in the house better, any-way, for I had a soft bed, and the flies and ants did not bother me there. I really felt sorry for "Two Spots" once. The boy at the hotel went out to the end of the pier and threw him into the water. My! I thought he was gone for-ever, because I did not see him come up, so I rushed in after him, and just as his head popped out, I grabbed him by the nape of the neck and dragged him safely ashore. Wouldn't you have been scared plumb through, boys? After that he would run to the edge of the water and back again, until one day he swam out with me; then after that he was a fine swimmer. I was always ready to rescue dogs or people, and one day I heard my master scream when he was in the lake, so I ran out on the pier, jumped off, and swam to him, took hold of his arm and brought him to shore. I heard them say afterwards that he was just trying me to see what I would do, but it is not right to fool any one about needing help when in the water.

One time out there I gave my mama a great fright. She was sitting on the bank reading, and supposedly watching St. Elmo, while my master and mistress went across the lake in a boat. When I spied them crossing to Catherine Lake, I looked at "Mom" (that is my master's pet name for his mother-in-law), and she was asleep, so I just quietly ran away and jumped into the lake and swam to the boat, so they had to take me in.   Every one on the place was looking for me, and they all thought I had been kidnapped.   Another day I was lost, so to speak, and all on the place started out on a search of me.   One boy went to the village thinking I had followed the bus; others went to the farms around; and even the good landlord was searching for me.   Where do you think I was that time ?   Playing baby upstairs in the hotel, lying on a nice white quilt upon a soft bed, and two little girls feeding me sugar and water out of a real silver spoon.   I was their sick baby and this petting was good enough for me.

I wonder if your mama would not enjoy this joke on my mistress ?   I shall tell it, however, and may be she will feel sorry for our poor family.   Well, this happened at the same place.   After I had been taken into the boat, we soon landed near a farm-house and after securely tying our boat, to a little twig, we walked to the house and introduced ourselves to the good farm-house lady, who was as glad to see us as if we had been her sixth-cousins.   We told her that we desired to take some nice crab-apples home with us so as to make jelly. She told us to help ourselves.   I took only one and ran off with it, and had a ball game all alone.   After my family had picked up two sacks full of beautiful crab-apples and were tired after such an exertion upon a warm day, we prepared to return, my master having insisted upon the farm-house lady's little farm-house daughter accepting fifty cents.   You know the good farmers do not like to take money from tourists for anything they want, as the visits seem to give them so much pleasure, for they lead such a lonely life.   We pulled for the hotel and got there a little late for luncheon, so we had to take what we could get.   My master then got one of our trunks out and put the two bags of crab-apples into the bottom of the trunk.   That was all right, but that mistress of ours always has her own plans and ideas, which, to keep peace in our family, we are obliged to respect.

So she thought we might as well send home our gas-stove, which we had had to keep us warm in our summer-rooms. *She* thought best to place the stove in the bottom of the trunk and place the bags upon the stove; so out came apples, and my poor master was warm and tired anyway (and just to think he had come up to the lake after a hard busy business week to get a rest over Sunday!); he got his rest later when he returned to business. After the stove had been lifted out four times and the bags seven times by my ''hen-pecked'' master, the boss thought it was ready to go to Chicago, so off it was shipped that very day. Now, it was obliged to remain two days in the freight-house by a mistake of our teamster and a week longer in our basement awaiting our return and the jelly-making. Of course we went down to see our beautiful crab-apples as soon as our inspection of the house had ended, for my mistress had all the closets to look into, all the cubby-holes to peep into, and above all she had to look under every bed, just because she was a woman, so at last we got down to business. Well! I can not describe this scene. Ask your father if he ever saw your mother look into a trunk filled with crushed crab-apples, making cider by themselves. This was the picture, but my mistress's face no one could have ever painted, for it changed its poses so lightning-like that I was dazzled at the wonderful kinodrome in her usually calm face. What a difference in a picture of ''before and after taking.'' The trunk was so stained that our washer-woman fell heir to it, and the stove was so rusty that,—well, we are still heirs to the stove. Then my mama had to have a hand in the packing, so she at the last moment had placed her cape lined with lavender satin (just think how stylish it would be now) on the top of all, and when she found the cape, it had cuddled down under the stove so closely that the name of the stove was perfectly printed upon the lovely lavender lining, so no one fell heir to the cape. Oh! yes the rag-man did accept it. When my master got home and he saw the scrap that the crab-apples had had, he sat down and yelled, and the louder he laughed the madder my mistress became, until I really thought there was ''something doing to beat the band'' (one of master's pet expressions). When any one says ''crab-apple jelly'' now we all turn pale. If *your* father laughs I feel sure he will hurt my mistress's feelings.

There was a very nice family living near the hotel, named ''Bucks.'' I ran away down there several times and they fed me cake and let me lie down on their parlor carpet.

I had another fine place to visit, and that was ''Mc-Ginty's Farm''; such good people lived there. They gave us apples (I like apples with their skins off), and they gave us fresh milk from their moo-cow, and nice well-water to drink. They had some funny things on two legs on their farm. I never had seen such strange animals; they had mixed-up names. One day I heard them called geese, next time they were gooses (when a little boy spoke of them), and again they were called goslings; so how was I to know how to address them ? One day when I had strolled up there all alone, I went up to one of these funny birds and as politely as a young man could address a young lady, I said, ''How do you do, Miss Goose ?''and what do you think she did ? She just ruffled up her feathers, stuck up her nose, and started for me. I fled. I had insulted her. She was Mrs. Gooses, I suppose, and did not like my dropping the second syllable. Later my master said she was protecting her family, a dozen of the ugliest little bead-eyed, yellow goslings that you would ever wish to see, and she thought them just too sweet for even me to look at. To tell the truth I was aching to feel their fluffy dresses. My mistress used to take them up and rub their soft down against her face. How she does love everything that has life in it! She wants to live on a farm, and so do I.

I was sauntering again one day by the babbling brook

when I heard "gobble, gobble, gobble," and turned to face
the most vicious looking two-legged talking-machine I had
encountered thus far in the walks of life.   I did not ask his
name, but ran home, never turning to see whether he was
after me, and I cuddled down on my bed, shaking my very

"THEY HAD A WAY OF MAKING THEIR HAIR FRIZZ UP"

teeth almost out.   I never passed that way alone; but about
a month after, I was with my master, and I met another
creature just like the first, and when I started to go back my
master said, ''That is only a turkey-gobbler, he will not
hurt you if you let him alone.''   I took his word for it, but
kept close to my master's heels just the same.   I think, however, had he opened his phonographic mouth and said ''gobble, gobble, gobble,'' I should have dropped dead.

What a dear little friend I had all to myself! She lived under the sidewalk. I never heard her name, but she was a little sister of the rabbit family. She was small, with a white soft dress with black on it, and she was indeed very pretty, she seemed very timid, for she would not let any one pet her, but was fed under the walk each day. How strange it was! She would come to the edge of the walk and put her nose up to mine for a kiss, and we were such good friends, but she never would let the other dogs come near her. After awhile they found two more sisters for her, so she was not so homesick. I always feel sorry for anything that is home-sick, for I have suffered many a day. This place was full of pets; one which I liked very well was a wee, pet chicken that was the particular pet of Marie's. This little tot used to delight in pecking my feet and in standing with all her weight upon my foot. She seemed to think I was made for her pleasure, so I just let her have her own way. Oh, yes! I almost forgot the three other pets, kittens, as white as snow, when they had not been in the coal-shed. These were very beautiful, but so very important that I could not get close enough to them to decide what color of eyes they had. They evidently had eyes, for they always saw me first. They had a way of making their hair frizz up and humping up their backs, so that they looked like a porcupine. (I saw one of these things later). I really like cats, but they shun my society.

CHAPTER XIV

The following summer we spent at Lauderdale Lakes. This place was another beautiful spot for children—and dogs.

Isn't it queer that any place that is nice for little people is lovely for dogs, too? I had quite a hardship in reaching this place. We went up on the train to Elkhorn, and my mama got into a stage and my master and mistress got on their bicycles and all started off on a dusty road. Poor me! I took "Shank's mare," and followed them all for seven long miles, awfully long miles; they must have been two miles to one, for when I reached the place of halt, I was almost dead. My tongue was hanging out of my mouth, my sides were puffing out and in like a blow-up balloon, such as you put into your mouth and make it squeak and puff out, and my poor feet! why, they were burned by the hot, rough roads, and the cushions were worn smooth and were as sore as boils. I was what the boys call "dead tired." Every one was very sorry for me; they bathed my feet and rubbed salve on them, and gave me a soft bed to lie upon, but do you know it was a week before I could run and play and be myself again?

How sorry my folks felt. They blamed themselves for not being more considerate. Of course they did not suppose that a dog would tire out before people. I being their first dog, all the experiments were tried on me. Seven miles is nothing for a dog to travel when in good training, but I had been walking on sidewalks and soft lawns, so I was not hardened.

After I got well, I found this place another jolly-go-as-you-please rest-cure. We stayed at the hotel one night until we could get into a cottage. We had very nice neighbors there at "Gorden's Camp," and some funny ones also. The strange and funny neighbors did not like me very well. The big, fat neighbor grunted every time I peeped through the fence at her, and after a few days when I peeped through,

GUARDING CAMP

what do you suppose I saw ? The funny neighbor with nine little funny neighbors all eating their dinner. These little piggies were only three hours old. After that day, I spent hours watching this curious family, but I had very angry talks with this spirited lady, for she used to tell me to go away from her beautiful darlings; and I used to tell her that I would not hurt them, that I was curious only to see what they were finding upon the ground, for they would spend most of their time with their noses in the mud, and I could not get into

the yard to see what was so interesting to them. Before I
left this lake (would you believe it ?) they were all big enough
to come to the fence, and be just as impolite as their mother
was, telling me to go away, and mind my own business.
This large camp was divided into sections, and the different
nationalities occupied particular locations.   Of course the
Americans had the
highest points and the
best surroundings; then
the foreigners, such as
the Alpine goats and
sheep, occupied another
high place; then the
cows and their little
cowies lived out of
doors all the time, with
a beautiful green carpet
under their feet; the
next nationality was the
"Plymouth Rock"
chickens; they seemed

PIGGIES THREE HOURS OLD

to visit around in the daytime, but at night they had a high
bed to sleep on in a clean, white house. But would you imagine for a minute they could sleep perched up on one foot
on a narrow board all along in a line ?   I really think they
were not of the nightmare kind of folks or they surely would
have fallen off and have broken their necks. I guess they
did not belong to the snoring family either, for they seemed
to be good friends.
    Near to the camp in the best house, next to the American
people's house, lived the next nationality; this was Arabian.
This high-strung, kicking, neighing, class of people was
known as "the horse family." Now, they were very useful
of course, to take the people through the country, so that they
should not get sore feet as I did; for you know horses wear

iron shoes. The horses were essential and deserved a good
home. Then there were neighbors unclassed, as I did not
learn their nationality. They were the frogs, the toads, the
bumble-bees, the spiders, the flies, and oh my! the very busy
mosquito. Another family that most folks did not like for
neighbors was the snake family, but they amused me the
most. I used to put my foot down on them, so that they
could not run away, and I would chase them all around, until
some big person would give a scream and make me stop
chasing snakes into her cabin. Now, these little, wiggling
animals must have been the "squatters," and have been
entitled to this land, for they drove every one away from the
spot where they squatted, and usurped all the land. They
were harmless little inhabitants and never talked back to
you, but just went on attending to their own business, for
they would not meddle with yours if you let them alone.
They seemed to be boss of the big folks, all right.

I nearly forgot the other charming inhabitants, the ones
all people love. The birds I shall mention first, they seem
to me to be the farthest away foreigners of all. They are
fond of building nests on the land, but go away to make their
calls, that is, they do not come near us, but they do sing
beautiful songs and help make the world cheerful. These
little foreigners are of a mixed nationality, and it would fill
many pages to assort them out for you, so as I am only a dog,
and not up on the history of flying-machines, I refer you to
the delightful bird-books. The other little neighbors, the
squirrels, I have the most fun with, for they are so cunning
and pretty. How they wink at me and tease me. One
minute they are sitting up holding a nut in their hands and
winking at me, then in a moment they are up a tree looking
down and saying, "How is that for high?" with the meanest
little sneer on their pretty faces, and with one eye closed to
show me that I am not the only foxy creature on earth. I
love to bark at them, and sometimes I stand so long looking

I am Posing for my Picture

up the tree, that my neck is stretched clear out, and it takes
hours to get it back into shape. But what fun! I am just in
play, and I think that they know it, only they like to tease.
What pretty tails these squirrels have and how nice they are
for fanning and keeping them cool in the summer time. The
chipmunks are my mistress's especial wild pets and she likes
to feed them, so she will not let me chase them away. I
can't have any fun with chipmunks so I never studied their
nationality; still I think they are Americans, for my mistress
seems to be partial to every one and everything American.

All these that I have spoken of were my most intimate
acquaintances, but we had some other neighbors who were
more like my mistress, and one lady in particular was very
good to me. She had a cottage a few doors from ours and
the first thing in the morning when I was turned loose, I
would go to her cottage and bark at the door. She never
sent a maid to say she was not at home, but always met me
with a smile and welcomed me as graciously as though I
were her dearest friend; and she *was* mine. When I walked
into her house I always looked on the table and went through
the pantry, and if I wanted anything I stood and barked at
it, and she always understood. I took possession of her best
couch in the parlor with lovely soft pillows and slept on her
best Turkish rugs; nothing was too good for me in her eyes.
She had a dandy little boy named Donald who liked me
quite as well as did his mama, so we had fine times together,
as you can see by our pictures in the water. I was there, but
you do not see me, for I was too large for the little hole in
the camera to paste me on the glass.

Donald had three playmates, Mildred, Hazel, and Sloan,
and we all went bathing together and sailed our boats. The
girls were twins and they were the cutest little girls that I
ever saw. Hazel could swim after her first lesson, and she
was only six years old. The children would blow up pillow-
cases and tie a string around the ends and use them for life-

preservers in the water; we used to have lots of fun.   Donald remembers us every Christmas, and some day I am going again to the place where he lives in the summer.   I do like good children.   I was sorry when school-time began for we all left the country.   We went to Elkhorn to meet the train there, and rode over in a hay-rack drawn by farm horses (nationality German).   The two trunks were in the back, and the two bicycles also, which I was thankful for.   Across the wagon was a board (my folks said after a few miles that it was a hard board).   Do you know what kind of board it was?

The two ladies of my family were seated upon this hard board and my master upon another (same kind) in the front of the wagon.   Then we had another occupant, a little farm boy, who drove us into the town.   My! what style!   The good farmer put a soft quilt down in the wagon for me to lie upon and under that was straw.   Just imagine a city dog being asked to sleep upon straw!   I graduated from that two years before, so I felt my importance and sat on the hard board between the two ladies until the rain came pouring down, then I was glad to get away down under the quilt, for if there is any one thing I dislike above another it is to be sprinkled.   I don't mind a good plunge all over, but I do not like to get wet in spots.   The family got drenched and they had to open the trunks at the depot to get dry clothes.   My clothes were all nice and dry, only my socks got muddy when I jumped out of the wagon.   I washed them myself so I made no trouble for the unfortunate ones.

DONALD, SLOAN, MILDRED, HAZEL

CHAPTER XV

Nothing happened during the fall and winter months in Chicago (it always seems a little slow when I get home, for Chicago is a quiet place for a dog), consequently I shall have to begin this chapter with my next outing at Eagle River.

We left on the fifteenth day of August in the evening. The berth that was assigned to me was in the baggage-car, and there I was once more chained to the radiator. This time, however, I had a comfortable bed, and a good man gave me water. I find lots of good men in the dog sleeping-car business.

We reached Eagle River the next morning at five o'clock; it was so cloudy and smoky that I thought I was back in Chicago. There was an electric launch waiting for us to take us to "Everett's Resort," about nine miles from the town. I must tell you what a little four-year-old boy called this boat—"a vaseline lunch." My master said he meant to say a gasoline launch. Well, boys, if you want to go to a jolly, fine place, where children and dogs hold full sway, and where the papas can catch real fish, go to "Everett's Resort," Eagle River, Wisconsin. The eating is first-class and the log cabins are clean and comfortable, while the jolliest inn-keeper that dogs ever saw keeps the place; he little knows that I am writing about him, but I want all the boys to know where this splendid resort is, way up in the pines, on a little peninsula, which is almost an island, surrounded by Cat-fish and Cranberry lakes, and where I was very kindly treated by the good landlord.

There were only nine dogs on the place. The tiniest was "Dolly," who was the size of my head; she was boss, and made us all "toe the mark." Next in size was

65

"Frank," who belonged to a guest; Frank was just the next size to "the boss"; then came "Smut"; he was so black his master gave him that name, but he was the hand-

somest of us all, and a step-brother to "Dolly."

"Nip" and "Tuck" were twins, both fine cocker spaniels. They comprised the firm of "Nip and Tuck Bird-Dog Company." "Nip" represented the social side of the firm, and "Tuck" the business end. "Nip" made friends with the hunters, found out their ways and traits, and gave the pointers to his partner, "Tuck," who handled the affairs of the company, leading the hunters or his customers to the right spot for game, and engineering the party through the tanglewood of the forest and bringing them safely home. At the sight of a gun he was ready and willing to head any army, but his social partner, "Nip," did not like

NIP

a gun, and refused to enter into any game that would destroy life. He had the same feelings as I had; he did not want to hurt anything, so we often discussed such cruel sport. Of course, "Tuck" made money—I think about a dollar an hour—and as there were many in a party they could afford to pay for their sport.

Every time a fisherman, or one who thought he was a

fisherman, would bring in a "muskalonge," the landlord would fire off a big cannon fire-cracker on the pier, and then every one would run down to see the "musky."

The game law in Wisconsin will not permit hunters to kill deer out of season, and I wish it never were in season, for these animals are so pretty and innocent, with such pleading, almost human eyes, that I cannot see how any man can slaughter one so trusting as they.

This is a wild country in the winter when the people go away, for the wildcats prowl around there and other small wild animals. One day three deer swam in front of our boat. They were crossing the lake, and when they saw us they were so frightened that they swam away from us, and landed on the nearest point of land. The first was the big deer, the papa deer, then followed the doe, the mama deer, and after her swam the cutest little fawn, the baby deer. This happy family had no doubt gone across the lake in the early morning to look for food, and were going home just at sunset.

It was a most beautiful picture and very interesting, as each one, as it landed, looked around, shook itself, and bounded into the dense forest. My mistress had her camera in the boat, but was too spellbound to take a picture. She says she had what the hunters have sometimes when they face a deer, the "buck fever."

CHAPTER XVI

When August came in 1902, I heard some talk about a vacation, and I wondered whether I was to go this time, for I did wish I were going back to see "Peg" or "Nip." When the trunks came up from the storeroom, I kept close watch for a few days, fearing that I might be left out of this trip (you see when my mistress goes away in the fall she leaves me at home); so, of course, I kept guessing until I saw my harness and chain brought out and left upon the trunk, which is always a good omen, for it tells me that I am surely on the list of fashionable dogs that are to spend the summer out of the city. Two days passed before the family mentioned the fact to me, still I watched the packing of three trunks, and when the third one was packed I knew that my master had had an invitation to go, for it contained just the things you boys would delight in—three fishing-rods, a landing net, reels, a big minnow-pail, a fishing tackle box with innumerable hooks and flies to lure poor fish; two pairs of old shoes, two suits of old clothes to supply the fisherman with dry duds, as they all seem to get as wet as they can—that is what my mistress says, but don't you tell. She throws his old duds away each year, and how my master stews around for a time, until he finds some clothes that will answer, for they must look as if they had had lots of use and real "fisherman like," you know. I had to laugh once when my master went way to the bottom of his trunk for an old "stand-by," as he called it, but I thought it was a felt slouch hat. Well, he could not find it, and he stormed around, and all the time my mistress, with a twinkle in her eye, kept saying, "Can't you find it, dear?" But "dear" never found that hat until he went back to the city, when he discovered it hung up in his den, for a curiosity. It was really a terrible thing for a gentleman to wear, all shot full of holes by a Winchester rifle. I used to see him throw it up in the air and shoot at it, but even now he longs for that hat every summer. My mistress is the real boss in our family, so she found him a better looking straw hat, but he gets so mad at it when he is out in a boat fishing upon a windy day, for, just as he is about to land a big fish, that clumsy hat blows off; and, as natural instinct tells him to let go and grab the old hat, which he does, he loses fish, rod, and tackle. He always said something to the hat, but I never understood what he said, and I was afraid to ask him to repeat it, as he seemed a little despondent at these times. Has your "pa" ever been a-fishing and had his hat blow off? Ask him. I'm real quiet when I go fishing. I never talk, as children do, nor do I scream as the girls, and scare away the fish. Some folks say that fish have no ears to hear talking, but that the women-folks are told that they have in order to keep them quiet in a boat. I like hunting the best, that is, the way that my mistress and I hunt. We take a gun and go away off into the woods and shoot at targets, tree-tops, old stumps, bottles, cans, and any old dead thing that we find, but we never kill anything on our hunting expeditions. We just look at the pretty birds, squirrels, rabbits, partridges, and the graceful deer. My master says that it is no fun hunting with my mistress, because if he kills anything she cries, and all the time she is wishing no huntable animal will appear, for he is a good shot. It is the same, my master says, when she goes fishing with him; all the time she is wishing the fish will not bite, so he has no luck, he says. But my! my mistress is the humanest person I ever saw. Why, she will not kill a fly; she opens the window and lets it go out, and just after it has been pestering me for an hour so that I could not sleep. Sometimes I think that she does not know that there is anything bad in this world; she often says she wishes that every one were good, and that there were no wars nor wickedness on earth, and no poverty.

One day when we were out in the forest, my master shot a partridge (my mistress called it a "poor partridge," so I guess that was the correct name). Well, I was sent to bring it to them, and I had to jump over bushes that stuck me, and crawl under logs, and I had a terrible time making a path. I found the "poor partridge," and picked it up in my mouth, but Oh! I dropped it, for it was dead, and it gave me such a shock. I had never touched anything uncooked in my life—all my meat is cooked—so, of course, it made a funny chill run over my long body, and the chill was so much harder because I was so large; but all pain is harder for long people than for short people, for the chill has farther to go in order to reach its destination. What a funny thing a chill is. It reminds me of an automobile running along, here in one place now, then, before you can catch your breath, it has fled. However, I carried the "poor partridge" by the wing and dropped it at my master's feet. I really thought he would feel sorry, but he didn't cry. You know men are not so tender-hearted as women. I hope my master will not ask me to carry his parcels again, for I want to obey; still, I cannot stand such shocks. I'll tell you a joke on my master, right here. The game-warden got after the hunters, but they did not catch him. We left the next day. The other fellows lost their guns and had to appear in court, but I heard they had been shooting all season without a license, so their guns were taken for punishment. People cannot disobey the law without being punished.

I started to tell you about my trip, and got switched off again from my first track. I have never written a story before, so you must bear with my shortcomings.

We left Chicago one pleasant morning on the Northwestern train, and traveled through a most beautiful country, passing Madison, the capital of Wisconsin, and her picturesque lakes. We got off at a place called Kirkland, on the shore of Devil's Lake, and were ushered into a nice little cottage right by the water's edge. I sized this up, for I calculated on having daily, and maybe hourly, swims. I was more than pleased. We all slept in this three-room abode, but my family seemed to be invited out to all their meals. As soon as a big horn would blow, they would go to the pavilion, where a lady filled them up with plenty of good things to eat. I was left in the cottage, and had my meals served there. I should have lots rather gone to the dining-room for my meals, but I guess my family thought that they were pleasing me and saving me the trip three times a day, for I did have to play very hard every day. They certainly had fine cooking up there, and all fruits and vegetables from the landlady's own farm. This lady was Mrs. Kirk, and she was very good to children and dogs. She gave me plenty of fresh milk and all I wanted to eat. We enjoyed that place beyond description, and we expect to go there again. The water in the lake is so soft it feels as if you are soaped all over. It is slippery feeling, you know. Then it is so clear that you can go in bathing and look down and count your toes. When we left for home, this good lady gave us a basket of luscious grapes, grown in her own vineyard, back of our cottage. This is a fine place to go, boys and girls. My coat was never so clean and glossy as while there taking my swims in this soft water; the sand on the beach, too, was so white and clean that I could use it for my bath-towel. It is an ideal place, and we all have a yearning for the "Kirk Farm." I will describe to my little readers, who have not been there, something of the beauties of this resort. The wonderful formations of the rocks, with their lovely coloring, is a picture that you will have to see yourself in order to appreciate it. I may show you a picture or two if I have space in my book. The pastures were fine, and the orchards with plenty of apples, dandy for boys; also

places for hazelnuts in quantities attracted lots of attention.
I used to go with the crowd, unless they climbed the bluffs,
then I was left at home.   And, if they only knew it, I could
climb better than any of them, for I have soft cushions on

TOMAHAWK ROCK

my feet which adhere to the stones.   The big folks say that
you can see all over when you get to the top of these little
mountains, and that the lake and everything else looks like
a small picture of a grand landscape.   One small bluff I did
climb, as my curiosity got the better of me, and there I saw
a big rock, just the shape of an elephant.   It was called

"Elephant rock." I was a little afraid of it at first, until I saw children putting their hands on it, so I went up and discovered it was a cold elephant, and quite tame.

I think you would like to hear about a friend of mine, a real personal friend, who lived here in a tent just for the

"A Cold Elephant, and Quite Tame"

summer. Her name was "Miss Guess," but, being familiar with her, I knew her as "Guess." She was really the smartest dog that I had ever become acquainted with in all of my pilgrimages. Her clothes were black and white, just in the latest fashion, and she had a beautiful bushy tail. I rather envied her that tail, as it was a fine fly and mosquito brush; and look at mine, no feathers on it at all—that dreadful wind in Kansas blew all mine off when I was a puppy. Well, "Guess's" family consisted of a master and a mistress and herself, just as many as in my family, lacking one, and they all lived in a tent and dined there, too. I used to spend lots of spare time there, and they were very good to me. I could fill the rest of the book with what they did and how they treated me, but I must not be partial, as other friends are waiting for their pictures and characters to be read. But a little about "Guess." Don't you see she looks smart ? She could add or subtract up to seven, giving you the correct answer in barks; she would tell you how old she was, and she did many hard tricks. The best and cutest, I think, that she did was to play the piano and sing. This is really so, cross my heart. One evening we were up at the camp, and it was pitch dark when we started for our cottage; so her master said in a voice just as he used to talk to us: "Guess, you go with these friends and show them the path, and bring the lantern back to me." Nothing more was said, and we started with the lantern, she running ahead picking the path. When we got to our cottage, Guess stopped in front of my master, looked up in his face, and waited until he put the handle of the lantern in her mouth; then she found the path and returned with the lantern safely to her master in the camp. She was the best trained dog we had met with, and the family always spoke to her in a gentle, kind way, saying, if she seemed tired, and they could see that she would rather not do her tricks, "Doesn't the little girl want to do her arithmetic ?" I had a chance one evening to get a little boom my way. You see, I had been spoiled so I did my tricks only when I felt like it. They never could depend upon me—I had to be just in the humor to do mine. So this night a company was on our porch and wanted to see and hear "Guess" perform. Of course, I insisted also, but she put her head on her master's knee and her paw in his hand, and looking up into his face with her soft, expressive eyes whispered, "Please excuse me, master, I am so warm and tired." So he did not urge her, as he said

Miss Guess

that she never refused when she felt well. She was a nervous, delicate little dog, and they never urged her. How I wish every one understood us poor dogs! The joke came in here: when she asked to be excused for not performing, I stepped forward and stood before my master, and offered him my paw, the right one, and he "caught on" that I was ready to do my tricks. So he asked me to count three, which I did; then he said, "How many are two and two?" I barked four times. Then to another question as to my age, I barked five times, for I was five years old; then I turned around and sat down in my master's lap. Again, my master held a piece of candy in his right hand and I barked one, so I got that; he held another piece in his left hand, I barked two for the left. I also ate that piece. I then sang for them in my loudest bass voice, and, after completing my performance, I was sent to sit down in mama's lap, which I did with a very satisfied feeling. How the guests all laughed, and my family was so tickled, as they did not pose me as a trick dog. But with all this, I still hold out that "Guess" is the smarter, for she must surely reason; so "I take off my hat to 'Miss Guess.'" I do hope I shall see her again, for we agreed so nicely. She is more beautiful than her picture, which is always the case when ladies have a picture taken. We bade farewell to our dear friends and to "Guess" one lovely morning, and left this enchanted place for Baraboo. Look on your maps and find this place. After taking in this little town we got into a three-seated bus and started over to a place where lots of brides and grooms spend their honeymoon (my family went there twelve years ago on theirs). This place is called "The Dells," and Kilbourn City is the fashionable place to have your baggage checked to, but we had ours in the bus, although when my family was on their wedding trip their baggage was carted to the hotel in a little hand-wagon. It was five o'clock in the morning when they arrived, and it was too early for the bus, so they had to walk two blocks to reach the hotel. That was not very stylish when they were on their wedding trip, I imagine, but it had to be done. Others suffered the same mortification. Just to think! Upon the first morning of your honeymoon, when you want to show how very important you are, to take your sweet, trusting bride to a hotel following her trousseau in a "Saratoga" on a wagon drawn by a small man. Was that not swell? The family seem to think it a great joke now, for they often laugh about that trip.

On this ride over to "The Dells," we had the benefit of some charming scenery, but lots of dust. My master engaged a three-seated omnibus so as to take out one seat and give me a place to lie down. Do you think I could lie down when we were passing so many sights — such as farms, cows, country dogs, and all sorts of things? So I just ignored the place allotted to me, and crowded between my mama and my mistress, and sat down on the seat. I never can avoid seeing all that is going on. After we had gone a long way we stopped at a farm, and all got out. I was glad to straighten out my legs again, as I felt rather stiff riding so long. This time we stayed at "Berry's Farm," or "Cold Water Cañon Farm," as some call it.

This was another place where we had fine table-board, and where I got plenty of fresh milk. I like good milk and I am very thankful that they analyze all milk in Chicago, for I have to drink different cows' milk there. We had another cottage at this farm, and I was extra happy, for they had so many cows, calves, horses, and chickens that I was very busy getting acquainted with their ways. It is so queer to me; each cow seems to have her own idea about dogs, and one never knows quite how to approach her. My mistress seems to understand their language better than I, for she walks right up to them, scratches their heads, and puts her arms around a cow that makes a face at me and runs with her horns to the ground after me; for my mistress seems to boss even a cow, and cows are generally bossies. My mistress goes to the "Zoo" and pets the big lion, "Prince," who lets her scratch his back. She is painting his picture, and if it is good I will show you a picture of it later, for he is a handsome lion. The lady on this farm was very kind to me, and to all children. The calves being so young they did not know what kind of four-legged animal I was, so they would stand as if dumb and watch me with great curiosity. You see, some folks say that I look like a calf, being the color of some "Jerseys"; so the little children-cows did not know but that I was their brother. Their "mas" always knew what I was. Other people say that

Two "Bosses"

I look like a deer. What *do* I look like, little people?

"The Dells" is a most beautiful place, and I shall try to show you some pictures of the rocks. The cañons are very cool and peculiar, winding in and out, with beautiful mosses and foliage about; even ferns grow from the rocks and make charming pictures. It is a treat upon a scorching day to rest in one of these beautiful, cool cañons, away from the noise and worry of life. And in these restful spots my thoughts turned to my own life; and I collected my first fragments of this little story for you, dear children, there in those enchanting dreamlands, with the birds singing their happy songs of welcome, the crickets and katydids chirping their thankfulness for nature's beauty, and the cunning squirrels and chipmunks playing hide-and-seek amongst the beautiful ferns. Then listen, the restless river flows on and on, reminding one of his life as it ebbs on. Sometimes, as smoothly it flows, one thinks of the beauties and peace of

"MY THOUGHTS TURNED TO MY OWN LIFE, AND I COLLECTED MY FIRST FRAGMENTS OF THIS LITTLE STORY FOR YOU, DEAR CHILDREN"

life; then again, of the turmoil, as the river rushes in mad frenzy and furiously spends its force in the greater "Father of Waters," ending its life in the Gulf of Mexico. It was when the river (the Wisconsin River is the one I am speaking of) was in a happy mood that we liked it the best; when we could see little sparkling bubbles that made us think it was happy. At these times we could sit and dream of but one side of life, the beautiful, the peaceful, the thankful, most thankful for all the glorious nature our Creator had bestowed upon all who could see the wonderful and appreciate His master hand in the creation of so magnificent a picture.

"THE LITTLE CHILDREN-COWS DID NOT KNOW BUT THAT I WAS THEIR BROTHER"

How I wish all tired-out men, women, children, animals, and dogs could spend a month each year in such a place; but if they cannot, how I wish they could see as much of nature as possible, and really learn to love the beautiful trees, birds, and flowers, and everything that can help to make the hardest walks in life easier for the weary feet.

This fascinating place, known as "The Dells," is where so many "honeymoons" are spent, as I hear the big folks tell about. Now, I do not fully understand about these moons, but folks say it is this way. A beautiful young girl (when

she is rich enough she is a "débutante," and if her papa be so
rich that he builds universities and libraries, she is then called
an "heiress"), well, she gets married to a duke (or any kind
of man with a handle to his name), and they are made man
and wife by a minister dressed in a long, white dress, with a

HANDSOME PRINCE, LINCOLN PARK ZOO, CHICAGO

book in his hand.   This is after all the fuss is over of getting
ready for a splurge.   She has been fitted to gowns until she
has no shape left.   She has attended dinners, teas, balls, the-
aters, until her eyes and head are dazed; she has had hand-
kerchief showers, pillow showers, tin showers, and china
showers until she has the real tear showers; then bonnets,
gloves, and every imaginable thing that can be bought to fill
the "Saratoga" is purchased for that sweet young girl to spend
weary hours in donning in order to appear charming, when,
if she but knew it, she would look much more bewitching in

a dainty, white dress with a simple flower-hat upon her pretty head. Well, after all this, comes the time for her to look her best, but she has dark circles around her eyes, and is a nervous wreck. So, after the ceremony, and after the rice has been showered, they go away to rest up and get acquainted, and to wonder whether it is worth while to get married. Of course, in their rush to the carriage, to avoid carrying away pounds of rice, and not to appear just married, they overlook the white ribbons and old shoes tied to their carriage, and only "come to" when they walk into their stateroom and find it all decorated with white ribbons and orange-blossoms, and notice that all the people in the car have a peculiar smile (not in the least interesting to the bride and groom); then, poor girl, when she takes off that lovely traveling hat, the porter appears just in time to scrape up enough rice to serve for dinner. I suppose the dining-car managers wish they had wedding parties every hour in the day; it is a bonanza for them. You little children may not understand all this about brides any more than I do, but if you have a big sister contemplating marriage, just let her read this, in a corner by herself, and then *she* will know what to do, so as to be smarter than her friends. You see, my mistress was a bride once, and I feel sure she doubly appreciates what I have told her here.

CHAPTER XVII

We left this enchanting spot and returned to the "contrasty" place, Chicago,—but don't you think that I do not like Chicago, for I still think her the greatest city in the world. Only, coming home meant to me formal walks, dog-catchers, muzzles, and lots of unpleasant things to contend with. As soon as I got home "Fritz" ran up to me, but I did not notice him. I was giving him a lesson, so that he would be more polite to other dogs. I meant to make up with him, however, as soon as I felt sure that he was sorry and that he understood his lesson.

I was glad to see "Jack." He lived on Prairie Avenue, and he was a beautiful cocker spaniel. His real name was Master John, but as we were familiar with him (that is, our family) we called him "Jack." He was as black and as glossy as the prettiest piece of black satin that you ever saw. He was very smart, but did not do any tricks, as his parents did not believe in making him anything but natural. He visited me a week, and I shared my meals and milk with him. I used to laugh at him when he drank milk. His long silky ears would drop into the dish, and I often wished that I could tie them up with red ribbons, and I guess he wished so, too, for he always had to wash his ears after a meal. Jack seems to love my mistress next to his family, and he nearly goes wild when she calls on him now. For, even after months of absence, he never forgets her, and makes more fuss than I do when she has been away. I am affectionate, but I do not show my feelings very much. So, sometimes my family say that St. Elmo is kind and loving, but does not seem to adore them as some dogs do their families. That is a mistake, however, for I do love them beyond description, only

84

MY FRIEND JACK

I have a way of my own in showing my feelings. I try to be manly and not too effeminate. Jack gave me a nice bean-bag for Christmas, and we correspond when we are parted.

Nothing happened worth mentioning that winter, so I shall continue with my next outing.

First, I must tell you what happened at my house on the first day of May. I went downstairs as usual in the morning after breakfast (I am not an early riser), and I found things in the greatest upheaval; everything seemed alive and tumbling over each other. What a topsy-turvy mess things were in, and what on earth were they doing? Had everybody and everything gone mad in the night? Even the pictures seemed to walk right off the walls. My! but this was a puzzle for me, and it was made worse when my master came down, and sizing up the situation, exclaimed, "What in the world will you do with all this truck? It will take a whole storehouse to hold this rubbish. I guess I'll go to my office. Good-by!" I wished that he had invited me to go with him, for there was no place to go, no place to sleep, no rugs to lie down on. What a friendless sort of chap one is when moving-day comes! I waited at the dining-room door until my mistress came through; then my eyes nearly popped out of my head, for she was dressed so differently from anything that I had ever seen her togged up in. I was sure that she had lost her senses, for she had a towel tied around her head, like a Turk; gloves, with the tips of the fingers cut off; and she was talking as fast as she could to three big men. I suppose she was bossing them. After things had cooled down a little, my mistress sat down on a box and thought a while. Then she said to my mama, "It may be that they will not take St. Elmo." My! did your heart ever sink way down into the toe of your boot? Mine did. I commenced to ponder. Was I to be left in this desolate house, with the furniture all scrapping and appar-

ently throwing things at each other? I never felt so blue.
Ask your little dog and yourself, and above all your papa,
how he likes house-cleaning time, or especially moving-day.
My master returned at noon and took away my mistress
with him, so that settled it for me. I was simply heart-
broken. I ran upstairs to see if they had taken "mom."
She was still there, packing her trunk. I was thankful
that she had not been invited. I always watch at the
window for my master in the evening. I know the time
that he gets home; I just feel it, and the family often wonder
how I know the time. The time-piece is inside of me, and
tells me when to look for my master, just as the thermom-
eter in my stomach tells me it is time to eat. So, at the
proper moment I was at the window, when, to my joy, my
two owners appeared. (I think they form a partnership, too,
just as "Nip" and "Tuck" do. My mistress attends to
the social end, and my master the business end.) As soon
as the door was opened I sprang to them, and the first thing
my mistress said, was, "Well, St. Elmo, we have found a
place for you where they will take Dogs." Isn't it a conde-
scension to take us to board? But I must not be sarcastic,
as I have been very fortunate about having good landladies.
So we boarded for a year after that upheaval.

We boarded on the South Side, by the lake, and I spent
lots of time in the water and in visiting Jackson Park. It
was here that we found some poor homeless dogs. People
said that they probably had been taken by unprincipled
men and boys to sell for vivisection purposes, and that they
had got away before they had been made prisoners. My mistress is very much opposed to the practice of vivisection, and
she helps all the unfortunate dogs she can. So I brought
home one day to the boarding-house a stray dog, his sides
nearly meeting with hunger. My mistress gave him some
warm food, also a bath, and after keeping him a week, she
found a good home for him. He was a pretty dog after he had

been cleaned and had fleshed up a little. He now resides in
Englewood. We named him Pinto. Here is his picture, after
a week of kind treatment. How he loved my mistress! He

GRATEFUL PINTO

would put his paw into her hand and rest his head on her knee,
and look up into her face with such grateful eyes, that even
a dog would cry to see how thankful he was to be treated
kindly. This was the second dog that we housed that
winter. This one we did not ask the police to find a home
for, as we did not wish to get again into the papers; but the

first little stray fellow I brought home got his name into the paper. It was a joke on my mistress, but it found him a good home. I will let you read what the "Daily News" wrote up. Of course, you know he did not play "Ping-Pong." This "write-up" brought many persons to the police station to get him, and some came in carriages. My mistress also got letters asking for the dog, and telephone messages. She replied to each personally, and asked that the interest might be taken in other stray dogs and cats who were not so famous.

PING-PONG DOG'S FATE

[From the "Daily News," December 18, 1902.]

Noisy delight in the game of ping-pong has caused Tinto, a trick terrier recently adopted by Mrs. William F. Senour, to languish in the Hyde Park police station until another kind owner shall claim him, and meanwhile Mrs. Senour is regretting the fact that life in one of the most fashionable of Hyde Park boarding-houses precludes the possession of a dog who will insist on speaking his mind.

Tinto was adopted by Mrs. Senour several days ago. Her beautiful English greyhound, St. Elmo, who has as kind a place in his heart for homeless strays as she has, brought the handsome little waif into his mistress's apartments one evening about supper-time, and showed by every action that Tinto was welcome to share his bed and board. After supper St. Elmo was put through his regular drill of telling his age, counting and performing sums in addition, when Tinto was noticed to be uneasy With a sharp little bark, he ran to the ping-pong table, and, jumping upon it, seized a racket in his teeth. His newly found mistress tossed a ball across the net to him, and, meeting it full with the surface of the bat, he returned it across the net. The joy in the discovery of a new trick for dogs was general in the Senour apartments, even St. Elmo, who is usually very quiet, entering into the spirit of the thing. In the heat of the game, however, Tinto would bark, and that was the beginning of a very sad story. Tinto, who was fond of looking at the lake from his mistress's window, would bark his delight when an especially large breaker would dash its foamy crest high over the break-water.

The end of the matter was that Tinto had to be banished from the society of the select and exclusive, and his mistress, in despair, took him to the Hyde Park police station in the hope of finding a good home for the little pet to which she had become so much attached. The first time she took him over, Tinto begged so hard to go back with her that she yielded, and again smuggled him into the forbidden domains. This morning, however, she bade him a final adieu and left him with his pet base-ball, which entertained him when not playing ping-pong, together with a box of crackers, and intrusted him to the care of Sergeant John Hogan.

Tinto was suffering from a ping-pong ankle, and he was tenderly received by the police officers, who promised to do all in their power to find a good home for the little animal, and sent out a message in the hope of finding the original owner. Tinto's occupation now consists of playing base-ball with the reserve force and eating the supply of crackers left by his mistress.

"Tinto" was a little "dachshund," black and tan, with very short, bowed legs. He evidently had been allowed to stand upon his feet too early in babyhood. My mistress did take him to the station, and the desk sergeant said he would find a good home for him, so my mistress turned to go, when she heard a little voice say, "Please don't leave me," and looking back she saw "Tinto" sitting up on his haunches and looking with longing eyes at his new mistress. She of course could not leave him after that, so she brought him back home, and the next day she had some one else take him to the station, where after the notice in the paper he found his rightful owner. Many thanks to the "police officers" and to the "Daily News" for interesting the public in homeless animals.

CHAPTER XVIII

The next May we went to a beautiful suburban village, where we now live. I like it the best of all, for I can run all day without a muzzle and every one is kind to me, even if I do run into their houses without an invitation and look all over their dining-room table for their cream-pitchers.

The first thing my mistress did was to take me to the Town Hall and register me a two dollars' worth. She made me tell how old I was, which was six years old last Fourth of July, you remember. I was sent a bright tag stamped No. 1, which meant that I was the first dog registered. You see I am a citizen of the village now, and I have to pay two dollars a year to help support the town, which I am only too proud to be allowed to do. When I was boarding here the year before I was an honorary member of the village, so I did not pay taxes and I appreciate the courtesy bestowed upon me.

When we first came here, we boarded with such a good lady, as we could not get rooms at the hotel, it being filled. This lady took us as a favor and we stayed until our house was ready. She let me sleep on a nice, soft lounge in my master's bed-chamber and gave me good things to eat; so I dearly love her, and when I see her, I jump up and kiss her on the cheek. My family say they cannot understand why I kiss her and no one else, but I will tell them here: it is because she let me go to bed in the evening with her little boy Dexter, and when the big people went up to bed they found us each night asleep together; each one had a pillow, and how I did enjoy this. I'll tell you a cute thing the little boy used to do. When he was sent up in the evening to study his lessons, he would say, "May St. Elmo go up to my room while I study?" and my mistress would say "Yes." So up I

92

would start, but did we study any lessons? Ask this boy friend of mine. We always went to bed tired, so you can guess we had a romp. He was very good to me, and so I am always glad to see him. I was pleased when I found out we were going to have a house to live in, for I like an upstairs to a house since I have learned so well how to climb.

The first day I entered the new house, I was a little disappointed, as I saw nothing but bare floors and walls; but the second day I found to my delight the same old boxes, barrels, pictures, furniture, and rugs, and this time they all looked peaceful and orderly. My mistress was beaming with happiness over the meeting with her old possessions, making a "contrasty" picture to the one of the May before when the hurly-burly impressionistic picture was painted, never to be effaced from my memory, when everything was on the warpath. "Moving-day, May, 1902," is the title of this painting.

Our house is just a little distance from my boy friend's, but I never am allowed to go there alone, as the "Choo-choo" car tracks have to be crossed to go there, and the family always hold my collar for fear that I shall be run over. Imagine a big dog like me having to be directed where to go! I do feel so silly, especially when the children, or other dogs are passing. When I had been here a month, I cut my back on a barb-wire fence (such a fence should be condemned), and my mistress thought I had been bitten by a dog; so she hurried me off to the train; but there was no train to Chicago for an hour; then we went to the street-car line, and the conductor said that dogs could not ride on these cars; after a few seconds of pleading, however, I was pushed up some steps into the car. My mistress paid five cents for me, and the man pulled a bell to say that I was paid for; but I had to stay on the back platform, and my mistress stayed with me, for she is very faithful to me. We then got on the elevated train, and I rode in the car, sitting on a seat and looking out of the window. It seemed very funny to be whizzing along in the air, and I wished that Klondyke could have this experience with me. I did not feel quite certain of this flying machine, and when it made me go from side to side, I had the same dizzy feeling that I had when I took my first ride on that IRON HORSE. My! but I have learned lots since the first day that I left Kansas, and I do wish that all the dogs of that windy place could learn as much. I have a tender spot in my heart for Kansas, for it was bright and sunny there even if the wind did blow all my hair off.

Well, I got into Chicago and down to the veterinary surgeon who examined me one dollar and a half's worth, and said it was no bite, only a cut by wire. I knew how I got it, but my stupid mistress could not understand me. She was greatly rejoiced, and telephoned my master to come and meet us and take us back to the country. I forgot to tell you that I had two severe operations at different times, and two tumors removed from my knee by this splendid surgeon, Doctor White, and he said that I was a hero, for I stayed on the operating-table, and they did not have to tie my mouth. I watched his performance and tried to think it did not hurt, as I felt sure he was doing it for my good, so I was patient. Let me tell you how I got those horrid bumps. In our Calumet house was a window bench just wide enough for me to lie on, and such a splendid place to see all that was going on outside, and still be on the inside away from the flies (when I say flies I shake all over). The family had it nicely padded when I came to live with them, but after my constant camping on it, the cushion wore thin, so that every time I jumped down I scraped my knees and soon made a lump; then again, I had to wear a harness when I was going on a trip, and when I would lie down the buckle came where my knee did, so that also helped to enlarge this bump. My family did not know this or I never should have suffered, for as soon as they found out what caused my troubles, they had a new window cushion for me and the hard buckle changed, but not until I had cost them a "twenty-dollar william" for operations. My harness was made where they made harnesses for horses, and it was all right at first, but I grew so fast that the buckle could not keep up with me, so we became a misfit.

There are some very nice and polite dogs out here. My very particular friend is "Captain," a brown setter. We understand each other and have great sport. My nearest neighbor is a brown water-spaniel, "Brownie," but he is a little particular about getting acquainted too soon; so we just speak. I think he is a wee bit jealous, as he has a young master and mistress who are very dear to him, and he does not want any one else to share their petting; then too, he was here first, and "possession is nine points in the law," so I have only one point. Well, we do not quarrel, and as my family and "Brownie's" family agree, of course we shall some day be friends. I shall, however, ask him to my next birthday party, but I hope he will not bring me a woolly-puzzle dog. "Buster Brown" gave me a pointer on how to have parties, so I am going to try it next time, only I hope my presents will not be returned. I shall be "foxy" and tell my friends to bring me things to eat; so that they can be consumed before the time to return them comes. Let me think! I should like best of all a bone, for that is what I never get, as my family say that bones make me ill, and the doctor also said I could not have them as my digestive machinery inside was too delicate to grind up bones; next would come English walnuts, next cake, then candy, then ice-cream—I could eat about a quart of that, sure. Oh yes! I forgot vaseline! I am very partial to that; it's next to butter, which I think comes second in my likes. I have a good many toys. This Christmas I received in my stockings a rubber humpty-dumpty doll, a squeaky ball, a bean bag from Aunt Lillie, a new blue ribbon, and a bath. I seem to get baths on all holidays, so that didn't count as a present. When I first came out here I could not find my playthings because the family was so slow in unpacking my things; they thought mine the least important, but I considered them first; so I had to play with sticks until one day I saw some nice little children playing near our house. One of the children had something in her hand, and as I was very curious to see what it was (for at a distance it looked very much like my old woolly-dog, after the battle), I walked up to the wee girl and took it out of her hand and ran home as fast as I could. My! how she did yell; that was a funny thing for her to do, don't you think? When I got home, it was a poor, forlorn pussy-cat looking very much like my un-grateful puzzle-dog. She had no eyes, and only one ear, which made you think she was lopsided; her nose and mouth had united, but she had a tail, the same kind of tail that my poor doggie had. I was very careful about the workmanship of her interior, so I handled her quite carefully. My mistress tried to find the owner of pussy, but she could not, so she left her in plain sight on the walk for some days; but would you believe that nobody would own her? At last I took pity on her and brought her into the house and she is now on my mistress's desk as she is writing at my dictation to-day. I love her best of all my playthings, for I always did love the poor homeless animals the best.

CHAPTER XIX

I have enjoyed calling upon some cats, the ones you see in the basket; two of them were never agreeable to me, but the quiet little fellow would come up to me and purr, and I would stroke his soft fur with my nose. The one standing up was so very impudent, even rude, that she took the liberty one day to scratch me on my nose, so after that I never cared for her society. I had a little unpleasant experience with a dog when I was at the hotel, which I forgot to mention. There was a black and white cocker spaniel named "Dewey"; he was a small one, but very aristocratic, and he boarded with his family at the hotel. He had been there so long that he considered it his property and that every one around belonged to him, so when I came, as he thought an usurper, he snarled at me, and said in a very important way, "Go away from my home, you can't play in my front yard, I am boss of this place."

I went to my mistress and put my head on her arm and she told me not to mind the little dog, that he would soon get acquainted, and be more affable: he did not do as we had expected but took every occasion to remind me that I was intruding. I stood this for some days, until one evening, when lots of folks were out on the lawn and I was passing him, he turned and spoke unkind words to me. This time I was not in the best of humor, so I turned and said to him "Boo! Boo!" He was very much surprised because he had thought me timid, but after that he grew quite polite, and soon found the way to our rooms when he wanted a drink of milk out of my bowl, or some of my dog biscuits. He is a neighbor of mine now, and a real nice little sort of chap, so I shall invite him to my party. I must show you a

picture of "Quentin Durward," for he is a particular friend
of mine, and a most beautiful collie. His nationality is
Scotch, and he was the next dog after "Dewey" that I knew
out here. He was polite to me from the introduction, which

"SHE TOOK THE LIBERTY ONE DAY TO SCRATCH ME ON MY NOSE"

was on the street. He took me to his house, asked me upstairs and all over, had his "mama" give me cookies and
milk, and was very kind. We went out to play in his large
yard, and after a time I wanted a drink, so he took me up on
a neighbor's porch where they always kept water for their
dog and showed it to me, then he stepped aside, and I took
a drink, and after I had finished he took his drink. This
is the truth; he is very polite about everything, and he is the

prettiest collie that I ever saw. He sleeps at his master's
bedside and goes to sleep with his paw in his master's hand.
Another reason why I enjoy life out here is because I can
ride around the country, and I like that much better than
walking. I usually have a seat reserved for me, and if I am
not invited I feel very unhappy. One day not long ago some
city people came to see us and there was an odd number,

QUENTIN DURWARD

so I had to stay at home. I just stood at that window all
the time that they were gone, watching for the horse to come
back, and when it did, after what seemed to me hours, I could
hardly wait for them to alight, but I jumped right in and
occupied the whole seat. The two gentlemen were so
amused that they started up the horse and took me to the
barn, and they had to insist upon my getting out, for I did
want a longer ride so badly. You see when my family go
for a drive there is always a seat for me, as we are just four;
but when we have company and take a three-seated rig, I

am left out, and what is strange to me, no one ever stays home and lets me go in his place. Now I am speaking of myself again, I must tell you how I became the proud possessor of my name, St. Elmo. There is a beautiful book named ''St. Elmo,'' written by a charming author, Mrs. Augusta Evans Wilson, whom my mistress loves and admires more than any other author; so when she was fourteen years old she read this famous book, and at that time promised herself a greyhound, whom she would call ''St. Elmo,'' so you see I was named years before I came into this wonderful world. If you have never read Mrs. Wilson's ''St. Elmo,'' do read it as soon as you are old enough to appreciate such a delightful, beautifully written book. The language is perfect, and is an education in itself, with a moral, good and healthy, pure and beautiful. It is my mistress's great privilege and pleasure to correspond with this most noted author, and in one of the letters in which the writer speaks of me, she kindly says ''your noble St. Elmo,'' and ''your handsome St. Elmo.'' Now, boys, should not I be real good and kind when I am appreciated by one who is so renowned and beloved as Mrs. Augusta Evans Wilson? This is my tribute to this kind friend who bestowed upon me the beautiful name of ''St. Elmo.''

CHAPTER XX

Oh, yes! I almost forget to tell you a joke which turned out to be a joke on the other fellow. Well! I have a little bad habit of getting on the beds when the family is not looking; as they do not believe in whippings, they have a hard time breaking me of this careless habit. My master thought one day he would scare me "plumb through," so that I would never get on the bed again; he found me asleep there, and next to me my mama's Sunday hat-box (it was naughty, too, to be on the bed instead of on the closet shelf where it belonged); so my master took the clock, set the alarm carefully so that it would ring exactly at 6 p. m., and then went back to bed (for he had been playing off sick all that day, but he could not stand it any longer, and so he had to get into mischief); he then called my mistress who was downstairs and they both sat like geese upon the edge of their bed waiting for the frightful shock to my nerves. I was having such a nice sleep, dreaming of the country, of swimming, and of my friends "Nip" and "Tuck," when without a minute's warning, "ting-a-ling" went something at my ear, and I immediately guessed it was in that Sunday hat-box; so instead of jumping for my life, I merely stretched my elastic neck (elastic is the polite name for rubber) and peeped into the box, but to my dismay it would not stop. I then looked into the next room at my giggling family and saw that they were too stupid to help the poor clock out of its sufferings, so I peeped in again, and it recognized me as a friend and stopped crying. I then put down my head and was in dreamland once more, leaving my disappointed family to conjure up in their mighty brains what scheme to try next. But what a joke on my family. I know they felt flat, and they could hardly look me in the eye that evening.

I had to go to the dentist's the other day and that made me good for a while; if there is any one thing I dislike more than another it is dentistry. I should not mind it so much if a gentleman in a clean, white linen jacket, who seemed to be the business end of a machine which buzzed like mad, did not put it into my mouth. Whizz! I never knew whether my head was whirling or whether the world was twirling, whirling around, it felt like a "merry-go-round" at a circus. With the first whirl you lose your breath and wonder where you will join it again. It is quite fashionable to have your teeth filled with gold and diamonds, so of course we must suffer a little to be fashionable, even in the canine four hundred. My teeth are not filled, however, for I only had mine cleaned, so I do not possess any gold or diamonds in my mouth.

I met with a small accident last Tuesday just as part of my family was going into Chicago for a luncheon. I stepped on a piece of something sharp and cut my third toe; it really did hurt, and of course the red blood dripped all over the porch, and my mistress was very much frightened. I tried to show her that I was sorry to keep her waiting, when the carriage was ready, too, but she would dress my foot before she left, and she told "Tenie" to take care of me, and if I grew worse to telephone my master or the veterinary surgeon; but I got better, and I think when my mistress arrived at the luncheon in the city she never thought of me again, for do you know she did not come home until after dark, and poor me waiting sick in bed for her. When "folkses" go to luncheons and teas you can depend upon their getting home just at the last possible hair-breadth chance. My! if I ate from one o'clock until seven at night I should be filled up for years, I'm sure. I hear funny remarks sometimes about places I have never seen

LOOK AT ME! TOGGED UP LIKE A GIRL

or been invited to. One place that always arouses my curiosity is the "club"; now, I hear that word very often, it seems oftener than I hear "church," and I wonder what a club is. Do you know, little people? Do your mothers go to a club, and do they ever take you? I believe children do go sometimes now so the mothers can tog their little tots up and show them off. Maybe it will soon be "Dog's day," then I shall surely be invited; my family is very proud of showing me off, dressed up to kill, with ribbon of the most delicate blue around my neck (my neck was not made for a ribbon display rack), and I always get it soiled, and I wish they would not make me look so silly. Look at me in this picture, dressed in a lace skirt and waist, with a blue sash around my waist, and a girl's sunbonnet.

" I MYSELF REALLY CAN SEE THAT I LOOK QUITE MANLY."

Now, that might do for the cunning "Miss Guess," but to dress a boy up like a girl is a shocking shame, and I think they should legislate upon this. I seem to be the subject for posery in our studio, and all the old hats and old clothing they want to preserve by the art of photography, they tie on me, and I am obliged to support these fads. Now, this picture of me in a silk hat I do not object to, as I myself really can see that I look quite manly, and if you can see the cigars in my vest pocket you will discover that I am a smoker. Of course I would not smoke one for anything, as I am opposed to tobacco, and especially to the smoke, but the effect is there. They tried to make me hold a pipe in my mouth, but this I positively refused to do. That might be all right for tramp dogs, but not for educated ones.

CHAPTER XXI

I have just come up from my dinner, so I will continue my dictating to my mistress. Do you know that I am fond of milk, and in particular, of cream? There seems to be quite a difference in milks at our house. We have brought to us every morning milk in large bottles, and cream in small bottles. When I say cream, my throat seems to thirst right away, and I smack my lips. It is so good. They can't fool me either, for sometimes they give me skimmed milk. We get this milk in another way, that is, a milk-man brings some at night in a bucket and this is set away. In the morning the cream is taken off and the thin milk is left for cooking and for me. But don't you think for a moment that I drink it, for I graduated from skimmed milk many days ago, and unless I see it poured out of a bottle and unless it is rich as my family use, I never accept any milk. Sometimes the ladies of the kitchen try to fool me, but the joke is on them, for they have to wash just one more dish, as I never wash it up for them, as I do when pure cream milk is given me. But what I do like to get is real cream out of the best silver pitcher which is put on the table. Now, I know that the best goes there, so I often watch for meal-time, as I go to the table just as the family are about to leave it, and it works every time, for they haven't the heart to send me away without a little cream in a real china saucer. I am not allowed to go to the table, as my family think it is not the place for animals, but I lie down between the dining-room and the library, half of me in each room; and in that way I see what is served for them, and yet I am only part way in the dining-room. I do not eat what is left from the table as I am not a vegetarian, so every day my order is sent to the meat-

market, and I have fresh meat cooked each day. I live
like a king, so I should not complain. When I go away
each summer, although we board we always pay for my
milk and meat, and one year we had to buy ice to keep the
milk from spoiling. Milk has a way, you know, of getting
cross.

The way little children's hair is cut now-a-days reminds
me of something funny that happened when we were at Channel Lake. There is a farm near this place for boys who have
no parents or homes, and it is fathered by a good man who
was once a minister. The boys learn farming in the summer
and in the winter they learn banking and business, besides
having their school each day. This place is called "Allendale
Farm," being named for the founder, who tries to make
good men out of these poor, unfortunate boys. They earn
small wages for their work, and help provide the home with
vegetables from their farm. What a splendid charity this
is. When the boys spend all their money they have to go
without a "hair cut" or some pleasure until they earn more,
so as not to be beggars. As we understand it, the idea is to
carry on a business for them and they can borrow a few
cents, and then promptly pay it back, as soon as they earn
something. Now I am getting at the part that interested
me, and it makes me laugh real hard. This good father
wanted to give three of the little boys a day on the lake, as
they were not very well; so he brought them from Antioch
on foot to the lake where we were. After he had taken them
for a boat-ride he brought them over to the hotel to let them
look around. Of course you know that a man at a summer resort upon a week-day is a great curiosity, and is much sought
after by the ladies, so the first thing that the unlucky man
knew, he was surrounded by the fair sex, asking all manner
of questions as to his business at the lake. They examined
the boys and found that one had one side of his hair short
and the other side long. Anything out of the ordinary, as you

know, always interests the ladies, so after fishing around for the gentleman to tell them, they had to come out boldly and ask him. He said that the little chap had spent all his money and had only enough to pay for one-half of a "hair cut," and so would have to wait until he made more to get the other side cut. Wasn't that funny? He did not have to wait long, for after they had all been invited in to dinner by the landlord, the gentleman thought he would cut the other side, for it would not be kind to make the child a mark of ridicule, which was very noble indeed of the man, for it is never kind to ridicule any man, woman, or child (only animals). But this father of the home did not know how to cut the boy's hair, as he had only a man's scissors, which is a pocket knife, and that would hardly do a nice job; so seeing my mama in her window, and knowing she was a motherly person, he quietly asked her if she would lend him her scissors, which she did, and had the little fellow come into her room, and it was turned into a tonsorial parlor before a bat could blink its eye. The boy promised to pay the gentleman for his hair cutting as soon as he could. I think these boys are not permitted to take pennies as they are taught to work and not ask for help, so it was a strict business loan. I think it costs five pennies for one-half a hair cut. The boys all seemed very happy and a great many of them are taken care of at this farm. It would have done your heart good to see them eat, that day. I peeked in at the window several times as I was in a hurry for them to get through in order to play some more with me. The dining-room windows were built just to accommodate little people, so I could see in and watch others eat. It is a pleasing sight when one is not hungry. Well! when the ice-cream was brought on, you should have seen the little-half-hair-cut-chap's eyes. They nearly popped out of his head. He raised up in his chair and looked around to see if the ice-cream was coming his way. I rather looked that way myself, for ice-cream is one of my favorites. He got some, but I did not.   I just got a whiff of it once in a while as we played.   But he was happy so it made no great difference to me after I lost sight of the ice-cream, for fun comes first on my list.

A lady told my master the other day that I looked like and was marked the same as a famous English greyhound, named "Master Ma Graff"; that he had won many prizes in England.   She said he was tan-colored, with white trimmings just like me, so my picture was sent to England.   If the owner of "Master Ma Graff" ever reads this book I ask him now to please send my mistress a picture of his dog. We may not have spelled the name correctly, so please understand what dog we are asking about, and oblige St. Elmo.

CHAPTER XXII

I had another joke on a fellow the other day. I was walking along minding my own business, when suddenly there appeared, as if popping out of the ground, the queerest looking four-footed animal that I had ever cast my busy eyes upon. He stood about six feet from me (that is by my mistress's tape-line, which stretches), and he stood as stiff as that wooden Indian. My first thought was that maybe he was a cigar-sign too; then as my brain took a turn I recalled the Indian that *was* alive, so I thought I would take no chances, for which later I was quite thankful. I saw

WILLIAM GOATY

this stiff-legged beast wink one eye, then I knew he was very much alive. He appeared to be getting ready for an attack of some kind and I figured that I was the pleasant subject of his ire, as by this time he seemed to mean business, for he winked the other eye, and then both eyes. Presently when we had admired each other quite long enough, and as long as politeness would permit, he arose upon his last feet to a great height, and shaking his two hands, and tossing his haughty head, with one snort he sprang at me; but— something from within me gave me a gentle boost at the

111

same time, which, with my athletic training, landed me on the spot where my enemy had stood, and when my remaining senses came back I saw the uninvited enemy on the spot where I had been standing, almost glued to the spot. It

was the funniest sight that I had ever seen, and now that I can see the joke I laugh. Can you imagine a funnier sight than this mad, madder, maddest Billy Goat not finding me on the spot? He aimed all right, and had I been glued there what would have become of me is for you to tell. Well! Billy was very much surprised, and I imagine a little disappointed at not finding me. He smelt the ground, and then he scented the air (just as if I had been foolish enough to go up in the air), and finally he snorted so long that I really wondered how he could hold his breath all that time. I had no breath to spare as it was, and I was resting behind a bush and peeking out at him. My! I was never more tickled. He no doubt thought that I had melted away, for he kept looking for the grease-spot, so I let him think that I had melted. It is not always wise to try to change another's thoughts to one's own.

WHEN YOU SEE THAT HIS NAME LOOKS "BILLY GOAT," RUN! RUN! RUN!

After he had settled the matter as to my disappearance, he shook himself, and walked away to find a pugilist more of his style. I giggled until my sides ached. My mistress came out and found me very tired; so she sat down and explained goatology to me. She said that his name was Mr. William Goaty when he was refined, but that when he was a pugilist he was only Billy Goat, and that when you saw that his name looked "Billy Goat" to run! run! run!

CHAPTER XXIII

My! I'm laughing yet! What a funny little, old, dried-up fellow a monkey is. But a monkey does not look the same to my mistress I know, for she held one in her lap the other evening, and she was all togged up in a clean white dress. She made him climb the banister for a penny, and he took it in his shapely, left hand and with his right hand he took off his little red cap to my mistress and mumbled some Italian to me, which I could not understand. Well, that monkey could do everything. He took the prize away from "Dan," in waltzing, for his tail being longer, he made more of a sweep in turning around. Then he had on a pair of green baggy pantaloons that looked as though they belonged to his big brother, and on his tiny body he wore a red jacket trimmed in yellow, and a red cap with a blue border and a tiny black feather, signifying that he had "a feather in his cap," for his ability to perform.

While his master played the hand-organ he danced, shook hands, climbed trees, turned summersaults, and ate peanuts. He did have a wonderful amount of talent. My mistress told the man that the monkey was tired, so he let him rest, and we gave him a drink of water, for which the monkey thanked my mistress by taking off his cap, showing little boys and girls how to thank people for kindnesses shown to them. I was afraid my mistress was going to buy him, for she did not want the man to take him away. She has always said that she was going to have a lion and a monkey, and I heard my master say, "When your lion and your monkey come, I will go," and I am afraid that I shall go with him. I wonder whether he said that when my mistress bought me?

My mistress read a good article in the paper on the "Town Barn instead of the Hitching-post for Horses," that the kind women of Momence, Illinois, had completed such a barn by the assistance of the farmers' wives and daughters, and that the horses no longer will have to stand in the sun, and in the cold of the winters out of doors, as this large barn will accommodate all. I hope other places will follow suit, as this is a most humane act. Another thing that cities should have is a sufficient number of watering places along the streets for both animals and men. I noticed while in St. Louis that many large stone-bottom watering-basins were about the city and they looked as clean and as nice as the fountains and basins for gold-fish, and some were in the middle of the square. We have one at the entrance of Grand Boulevard in Chicago, but it is too high for dogs. We have often seen poor, stray little dogs try to reach up for water, so I hope that when other places for watering horses are being planned, they will be low enough for dogs and cats also; then when all lost or stray dogs can get water, we shall not have mad dogs. You know how dreadful it is to be thirsty, and with the animals it is more pitiful.

The birds need water in the summer more than they do in the winter, for then they can drink the melted snow. I wish that ladies would not wear the pretty birds upon their hats for show. It does seem wicked to kill the birds, or to kill anything just to beautify ourselves. Do not let anybody kill the birds about your town, for we need them all to help brighten the world. Remember that they sing for us songs of the happiness, the joy, and the bountiful goodness in all things bestowed upon us by our loving Creator, and that He made all that is beautiful in this world to make us better, so that we must see the good in this life and not look for the bad, helping every one and everything that is in trouble. We keep a pan filled with clean water on our lawn for the birds and animals, and we put bread-crumbs out each day. It is a pleasure to see the birds enjoy the crumbs; the blue-birds, the robin redbreasts, the blue-jays, and other pretty birds, also the disliked little sparrow (but we like them, too), all feasting together at one board. Sometimes we have quarrels to settle, but as a rule our large family agrees. My master says he is going to put up a sign in our yard for the birds to read, saying, ''No fighting allowed on these premises.''

CHAPTER XXIV

Oh dear! I am so extremely happy to-day. What do you think? I have found a real cousin, and I have just re-

MY REAL COUSIN "DAN"

ceived his picture. He is very handsome as you can see, and very aristocratic looking. His society name is Master Daniel Gratiot, and he hails from St. Louis. He belongs to one of the oldest French families of that splendid city.

Of course *he* has a long pedigree, so I am very proud to belong to him. I'll tell you how we are connected. Daniel's masters and mistresses are cousins of my mistress, so you see that I am a direct cousin to Daniel. Now that I know him I shall call him by his familiarized name. I can spell this word, but I declare I cannot pronounce it, for my tongue gets tangled up. Let me hear you say it; I shall listen——

Now "Dan" should be very smart for he has nine in his family to teach him smartness. There is quite a partnership, he being divided into nine parts, while I am in only a three-party partnership, and most of the time a *one* part partnership affair. My mistress is going to St. Louis to see "Dan" and the "World's Fair," so when she returns you will hear more about this cousin of mine, and some interesting facts about this great "Fair." How I wish I might go, but I have not been invited. I shall hope that they may need me at the "Fair" and that my mistress will send for me. This is May 15, 1904. I will close with this thought of the dog in general: Did you ever notice that dogs turn around several times before they lie down, and that they always mat down their beds? Their ancestors in the wilds and jungles were obliged to walk around their beds and places to sleep, as the tall grass and shrubbery made it hard to get a soft place to rest, so this habit has been handed down and is a dog's own legacy. My mistress says that "the same traits that human beings have are handed down from generation to generation, and if we could only inherit all the good traits of our ancestors and leave all the bad ones undeveloped what fine specimens of men and women we should make, and what goodness we should possess."

CHAPTER XXV

Hello! Hello! boys and girls! I am home again from the wonderful "St. Louis World's Fair," and, indeed, it is wonderful. I shall do my best to describe a little of this great exhibition; but to give you an exact description of its beauties and its art I must ask you to visit it yourselves as I did, for it is certainly beyond all pen and paper to picture this beautiful landscape.

After my mistress and my mama had left for St. Louis I felt very lonely all day, although our faithful "Tenie" came over every noon and took me out for a walk and played with me. She was very kind and seemed to feel sorry that I had been left at home. My master got home from business at six o'clock each evening and cooked my supper for me on a gas-stove and took me for a walk, so that part of the day was happier. The good meat-market man and the good milk-man did not forget me, for each day they brought meat and milk to keep me alive while my unkind family was "doing the Fair." My master was a long time cooking my meat at night, but I tried to be patient, for I felt sure that this was his first place as cook in a family; he seemed to be so very slow and awkward. He told some friends last night that he was not homesick until I went away, for then there was no one to talk to nor greet him at the door; so you see a dog is rather necessary in a family sometimes. How I laughed inside when a little fat messenger boy came puffing up to our door that Saturday evening with a telegram from St. Louis, which read, "Permit granted; if he can safely come, send Sunday morning, Caro." That "he" was "me," and I was just as tickled as that dog with two tails was. So, on Sunday morning off I started on the "Choo-choo"

118

DAVID R. FRANCIS, PRESIDENT   WM. H. THOMPSON, TREASURER   WALTER B. STEVENS, SECRETARY

WORLD'S FAIR, ST LOUIS
1904
LOUISIANA PURCHASE EXPOSITION

DIVISION OF CONCESSIONS AND ADMISSIONS

NORRIS B. GREGG,
DIRECTOR

OFFICE OF THE DIRECTOR

May 28, 1904.

To the Gate Keepers:-
                                                                            St. Elmo,
      This will be your authority to admit the dog which will accompany
Mrs. Caro Smith-Senour, the bearer of this permit. It will be presented
on Monday, May 30th, for which date only it will be good.

Norris B Gregg.

Director of Concessions and Admissions.

FORM 58—1 M-1-08-P   No. 273

St. Louis and Suburban Railway System.

St. Louis, *May 28* 190*4*

To Conductors ·
    Permit the bearer to transport *one* dog   on Front Platform of Cars until
July 1st 190*4*
Issued to *Mrs. A. F. Senour*
Address *Chicago, Ills.* *J. Mahaney.*
                      J.C.C.

cars, two hundred and seventy-six miles, to meet my mistress and view the "World's Fair." My mistress and dear cousin "Bert" met me at the train. They had a special permit to go out to the train through the large gates so as to take me from the baggage-car, where I had spent a most delightful day watching the telegraph poles fly by and gazing out upon lovely pastures with cows, horses, pigs, and all sorts of four-footed animals enjoying themselves, eating nothing but grass. I was thankful that I was not forced to eat greens. At first I thought that everything and everybody was hustling along at a great rate, but later, when I was jerked from side to side, I decided that it was the big IRON HORSE once more taking me away. I was very glad to see my mistress and made up my mind to watch her very closely. We stepped on a street-car and my mistress took out a piece of paper and showed it to the little big man with brass buttons on, who was boss of the car. After he read the paper he smiled on me and said, "Very well." Now maybe you know why he said it since you have read, on the preceding page my permit to ride on the street-cars. Well! the kind man on the front platform, who was always turning a crank, gave us his chair to sit on, so we turned it over on its side and made out of one seat, three seats; in consequence, our cousin, my mistress, and I had a front seat all the way out to the place where we were going, while all the other poor passengers had to sit inside the car and did not have half so nice a view; but then *we* had a pass you know. I thought the IRON HORSE was the swiftest flying machine in the world, but I struck one faster in the way of the "St. Louis and Suburban Railway System" cars. They are the busiest cars my family ever traveled on, but they are all right, I think. After a ride of about five miles, we reached our destination and we were welcomed warmly by the large family of cousins, that is, all but cousin "Dan." He seemed a little cross at first, especially when his family made any fuss over me. I tried to keep away from them so as not to hurt his soft feelings, but he talked a good deal behind my back, and did not love his cousin St. Elmo as we had hoped that he would. Of course I did place his little nose out of joint, for his family wanted to make me welcome, which they all did, and they gave me fresh milk from their pretty cow and did all that they could to make me feel at home; so I shall remember them all with the greatest of pleasure. Even dear cousin "Dan" commenced to show that he would have liked me had I remained longer. Poor little "Dan!" he had received a severe cut upon his right shoulder-blade from a barbed-wire fence or something sharp, and he had to be bandaged up, so he had reason for not feeling amiable towards a big, strong fellow like me; then again, he might have felt a little ashamed to be dressed up in rags before his Chicago cousin. I know I often feel that way when I am togged up. My mistress loves "Danny" (that is her pet name for him; she always has to have a pet name for everything), and he seemed to like the name, for he really took possession of my mistress and went everywhere on the place with her. He liked to get up in her lap, too, and go to sleep. I envied him, for I am so big that only half of me can get on her lap at a time; so by the time that a half gets to sleep the half that is on the floor left over is awake. That is why I often envy small dogs. "Dan" had many smart tricks, and his waltzing around on his hind feet was marvelous to me. He steps around just as a person does in dancing. He was more willing to perform than I was, for every time that I started to do my tricks for the cousins and would start to count three, "Dan" would chip in and I would stop; so we had a hard time trying to see which one was the most talented. However, I "take off my hat to 'Dan,'" for he can spin around like a top in his waltzing, which I should never be able to do, for I should knock down all the bric-à-brac and lamps in the

room.   I should certainly need an acre lot to do my waltzing in.

   I found another cousin, "Billy Beck," who had not been
spoken of before by my mistress.   She was given to the
family five years ago by the groceryman; so they named her
after him.   She was a cute little kitten then, and the name
just suited her.   She still retains the name, and is as independent a cat as can be, and one that any dog might dread
to encounter.   She must have been very pretty in her early
youth, but since the wars have been raging "Billy Beck" has
lost a part of one ear and the end of her tail; so she is a little
lop-sided, you see.   She is black as tar, and her only trick
besides eating is to lie down and roll over when she is asked
to do so.   She usually does this with a squeak, for her voice is
a worn-out soprano; still, we are delighted to own her as
our cousin.   She seemed to have the ways of all cats, for as
soon as she would see me politely trying to talk with her,
she would saucily frizz up her hair and spit at me three
times.   I found out that even "Billy Beck" could count
three.

CHAPTER XXVI

After I had been inspected by all the relatives on that Sunday evening, I was sent to bed, and the next morning, upon my calling at the dining-room door for my breakfast, I learned that I was to attend the "World's Fair" on that very day, Monday, and that I was to be very obedient, and that I should not be rude and poke my nose where I was not wanted (just as if dogs ever go where they are not wanted). So, after a good breakfast, my mistress put on my collar with a pretty assortment of colors, blue, red, white, and yellow ribbons, and I felt very proud, as these are the "World's Fair" colors, also reminding me of our country's colors, without the yellow. We walked two blocks to the entrance of the gate, and my mistress handed the keeper a slip of paper, which he read and politely smiled on me, for that was my *special pass* into the grounds. Now came a little difficulty. I had a pass, so I had to enter at a special turn-gate, and as my mistress was just an ordinary guest, she had to go in the general gate with my dear cousin "Bert," who was our escort. But the difficulty was soon overcome by one of those small urchins who is always ready to "carry your grip, sir," so, he wisely took hold of my chain and the gate-keeper passed me, not through, but under the turn-gate, as I was too long for the space between the gate-arms, and too tall to stand up and walk through, poor me had to get down and crawl under, not a very dignified way for a distinguished personage to enter so great a place. However, upon my return from the inspection of the grounds and the buildings, I was passed out through a private door, for, you see, the gate-keepers had all those six hours that I was inside to study out a way to make it

123

more comfortable and dignified for me to pass out, and I really did appreciate their kindness. Another thing which we both liked was the polite treatment of the guards, who raised their hats to us, and sometimes patted me, for you know they all had been prepared as to *my* visit to the Fair, and smiled at the thought of a dog having a pass to view this great exposition. Another pleasing attention showed me was by the beautiful "Cascade" and fountains, which started to play just as soon as I arrived in front of them. I noticed all these marked attentions, and I feel sure that my fellow-comrades will rejoice with me that one of their nationality has been so honored.

My mistress wrote the following chapter for my book, so I shall relate it as per her manuscript upon the great "World's Fair" in St. Louis in 1904.

Seal of Louisiana Purchase
Exposition Co.
David R Francis
Pres.

CHAPTER XXVII

"THE LOUISIANA PURCHASE EXPOSITION"

The "World's Fair" in St. Louis, 1904.

[The beautiful "World's Fair" pictures were presented to the author, and are used by the kind permission of the "Publicity Department" of the great "Louisiana Purchase Exposition" in St. Louis of 1904.]

Through the courtesy of Hon. David R. Francis, the president of this great Exposition, and Mr. J. C. Thompson, Jr., private secretary to the president, also the "Louisiana Purchase Exposition Company," I have been granted permission to present to the children from a page in my book entitled "Master St. Elmo," a fac-simile of the seal of the greatest of all expositions in the world. I consider this a great privilege, as this courtesy has never been extended to any one else, and I trust that all the children will appreciate with me this favor, and read up and study all about the "Louisiana Purchase," so when they visit the beautiful "World's Fair" in St. Louis, and gaze with admiring eyes upon the imposing monument, 100 feet high, with the crowning statue of "Peace" resting so gracefully against the blue sky, they will understand and feel the importance of this magnificent and gigantic undertaking, and the gathering together of people from all over the world.

This seal has upon it the head of President Thomas Jefferson, also a fac-simile of his signature, and as he was the President of our Country at the time that the famous "Louisiana Purchase" was made, it is a very appropriate seal, and I trust that each of my readers will understand why we, of all states in our Union, are so earnestly trying to make this great "World's Fair" one of the noblest events in the annals of the United States of America.

CARO SMITH-SENOUR.

The fascinating place around and in front of the "Cascades" is the most beautiful spot that I have ever seen. The water starts from a basin in the center of the magnificent

"Festival Hall," and flows down wide steps with green glass across the front of each step, under which electric lights shine, so that at night the water looks as if it were falling

LOUISIANA PURCHASE MONUMENT,
WORLD'S FAIR, ST. LOUIS

over steps of beautiful green moss. The water falls into the "Grand Basin," which is the largest lagoon in the "World's Fair Grounds." It was indeed a beautiful picture, with fountains sending up bubbles, and the wonderfully lighted "Electricity Building" reflecting its hundreds of electric lights into the depths of the artistic lagoon, with the red-sashed "gondoliers" plying the oars of their "gondolas," keeping time to the elegant music, and the little boats, in the form of "the swan," beautiful in its whiteness and its graceful gliding, and the "dragon" launch, the bright-colored "peacock" launch, with its wide-spreading tail, so attractive with the electric lights thrown upon it. All this makes one sit and wonder if this is really all real, or if one is in dreamland. An evening with the stars above and the stars below, around,

FESTIVAL HALL AND CASCADE GARDENS, WORLD'S FAIR, ST. LOUIS

and about the "Cascades and Hall of Festivals" is a picture never to be forgotten. It is stated that one million dollars was the cost of this great central spectacle known as "Cascade Gardens," and it is said that the water is brought seven miles from the Mississippi River to supply the fountains and the lagoons and the "Grand Basin" in front of the imposing monument of the "Fair," the "Louisiana Purchase Monument."

The Palace of Agriculture is indeed a fine building. It occupies more than eighteen acres, and is five hundred feet wide and one thousand six hundred feet long, with a cornice line fifty feet high, it being the largest exposition building ever erected for a single department. It has a conspicuous site, for, standing on the hill in the western part of the grounds, it looks down upon nearly all the other palatial buildings. This is a very interesting exhibit, comprising the needs of every boy and girl. The exhibits of corn are fine, as well as those of rice, sugar, beets, tobacco, etc., showing the varieties and best of each. The Missouri State exhibit is very fine, and the pictures portraying farm-life are so real that I shall try to describe two pictures to you, dear children. These are about forty feet long and twenty feet high, and are the largest grain pictures ever made. One of these pictures portrays a farm in Missouri with a wheat-field in which binders, made of wheat, are in operation. Then there is a pasture scene, with a herd of high-class cattle grazing near a stream. It is an ideal sketch. The cattle are made of corn-silk, cotton, and wool; the horns are made of corn-husks. The pasture is of real dried grass; the road of timothy seed; the fence of cornstalks. In the background the trees are of sorghum-heads, while those in the foreground are actual trees; the meadow is of grass and the foreground is of wheat, with a miniature mower operating in front of the picture, with the grass falling in front and rising as it passes by. This wonderful painting (for in color blending and beauty it is as much a work of art as is a painting in oil) is made from nature's own growth, and is one of the best studies of art that the great "Fair" gives to the lovers of art. It received one of the highest compliments which could be given to it. Some flying squirrels got out of their cages and took refuge in the trees, and built a nest in the fork of the front tree and made themselves a comfortable home, thinking that they were back once more on the dear old farm. The nest you can see in the grain picture. When you stop to think that every bit of these tiny grasses is tacked or glued on this big board, and that it is done so neatly that you cannot see how it is put together, you will surely agree with me that this is a wonderful display of art.

The second grain picture, quite as large as the first, is an accurate reproduction from a photograph, showing a six thousand acre corn-field, with cultivators to till one thousand acres of corn a day. I am told that this farmer raises more corn than nine whole states raise, and that this is the largest farm of its kind in the world. The picture is made about the same as the one described to you, and shows seventy-two men, seventy-two cultivators, and two hundred and sixteen horses and the owner, the gentleman who is eighty-one years old, in the foreground, all made of corn-silks, corn-shucks, and other materials, the products of the cornfield. It is said that when the owner viewed this picture, he could pick out each of his men and call him by name, the likeness was so nearly perfect. This picture was copied from a photograph, and the artist may well be proud of his splendid achievement.

As a moral lesson, let me tell you about this able farmer, and see if you little children do not respect such a man. This gentleman, who is now the richest farmer in Atchison County, started life with one ox and a wooden plow. For the ox he owed, and the wooden plow he made himself. He persevered in growing corn and in raising cattle, until he has nobly come to the front as one of the largest producers in the world. He has founded and endowed a college, and to-day he is eighty-one years old, a highly respected citizen, independent and happy.

The Palace of Art consists of pictures, statues, bronzes, and of the paintings of great artists, together with pictures formed of Japanese embroidery. Each country is splendidly represented in the art of her country, and the French pictures of great artists are very fine. (The American exhibit was not completed when I attended the "Fair," so I shall not be able to tell you about it, but like all other American enterprises, I am sure that it will be worthy of mention.)

The Palace of Education contains everything pertaining to studies, books of all classes, exhibitions of the workmanship of the children of the different schools, such as manual training, beadwork, basket-weaving, house-building, fancy work, dressmaking, drawings, painting, compositions, kindergarten work, and all that comes in the line of education, and many of the exhibits are fine, showing what little, deft fingers can do by training them. No doubt that some of you, my readers, have contributed to this splendid exhibition.

The Palace of Manufactures is a pleasing piece of architecture, and is the nearest building to the main gateway. It is entered under a grand triumphal arch. This structure contains all manner of dress goods, and great machines by which is shown the mode of manufacturing cotton, silk, and wool goods; also all styles of laces, bric-à-brac, jewelry, furniture, rugs, paper, buckles, buttons, shoes, clothing, and everything that is manufactured over all the world. The busy little Japanese have an extensive and most praiseworthy exhibit, having marvelous hand carving and inlaid work and beautiful vases.

The Italian exhibit is also very fine, with its bronzes and marble statues. Other exhibits are worthy of praise, but my space is limited.

The Palace of Machinery has many towers, and it is not only a handsome building, but also a useful one. The building contains the great power plant, and it is from this that all the power for lighting the buildings and pumping the water for the great Cascades is controlled. In this building may be seen all kinds of pumps, farming implements, and machinery used in every part of the world.

The Palace of Horticulture is a neighbor of Agriculture, and in this splendid building may be seen all the palatable things one may wish to eat—delicious apples and fruits of all kinds; also beautiful shrubbery, palms, and flowers. The large fruits of California, bottled for preservation, are most interesting to study. I forgot to tell you that in front of the Agricultural Palace is a large clock which lies flat upon the ground. The dial is made of flowers, and when the great hands point to the hour, a brass bell rings out the time of day; the bell is worked by machinery, and is very large, about the size of the famous "Liberty Bell."

The Government Fisheries Pavilion is a most interesting place to visit. All species of fish are there in glass aquariums alive and swimming about, and with the electric lights thrown upon the water; the fish look very pretty, as the different colors show so well. In the center of this pavilion is a fountain where two seals enjoy themselves in the water, and bask in the sun on the rocks. Here you will find tiny fish and large fish.

The Government Building is most attractive. The dome crowning it is gilded, and is ninety-three feet in diameter, with a magnificent group statue called "Liberty-a-Quadriga" surmounting it. This is the conventional style of adornment of the dome of such a building, but this quadriga, as composed, is what might be termed an unconventional spirit. At any rate it has a certain dash and freedom, which, despite the adherence to traditional forms and symbols, give an impression of originality and strength. The central figure, the Goddess of Liberty, stands fourteen feet high in the chariot in which she is drawn by four colossal horses. She bears a torch in one hand and an eagle in the other. The horses are guided by two nude youths, twelve

STATUE ON GOVERNMENT BUILDING, "LIBERTY-A-QUADRIGA"

feet high, whose figures express the vigor and energy of early manhood.

The interior is free of columns. This great building contains the principal exhibits of the United States government. In it you will see a reproduction of our "Man of War" vessel, the "government mint," represented in working order, cannons, guns, and everything pertaining to the army and the navy.

I fear that I cannot do justice to the magnificent Palace

of Electricity. It is, indeed, a palace, and fronting upon the "Grand Basin," as it does, surrounded by lagoons and reached by artistic bridges, it is certainly one of the most fascinating and beautiful places that I have ever seen. Groups of columns are a striking feature of its several façades, and at night when it is sparkling with its hundreds of electric lights, it is a coronet excellent enough to crown any kingdom, the greatest of all, our own.

I could write a book upon this splendid "Fair," but as my space is limited I shall not be able to describe all the fine buildings, nor the plateau of states, as I should like to do. Therefore with a little description of the state represented, in which St. Elmo was born, I shall turn the rest of his book over to him.

The commission of the Texas Building extended St. Elmo an invitation to register in his state, so, with his mistress's assistance, he registered "Master St. Elmo, Chicago, Ill., six years old, born in Texas, 1898."

The hostesses introduced him to the guests, and he was entertained with great respect. The Texas Building is built in the shape of a star, for, as you children know, that Texas is the "Lone Star" state. It is very beautiful. I should like to tell you all about the different state buildings, for they are all attractive. Each one is original and appropriate, so I am not partial towards the only state building that I am writing about—but Texas happened to be the birthplace of the hero of this book. My greatest pleasure was in viewing the flags of all nations, and in feeling that this great undertaking had brought together all the peoples of the world in peaceful sympathy and love; and with our own beloved flag flying on every building, I thought that never had there been a more beautiful picture, nor a landscape more picturesque than this land of little hills, with its natural scenery and artistic arrangement of palaces and lagoons. With the star-lighted canopy of blue overhead,

and the star-lighted palaces at each side, I felt that fairyland
had at last been found upon this earth. Of course you children have been taught in your schools what a "World's
Fair" is, and that it is to bring together all the peoples of
the globe, showing their different products, industries, dress,

TEXAS BUILDING, IN THE SHAPE OF A STAR

and customs. The oddest of these people are very splendidly
represented on what is termed "The Pike," in the grounds
of the great "Fair." This "Pike" is a wide street, about
a mile long, on each side of which are buildings and
reproductions of towns of foreign nations. For instance,
there are before your eyes the "Streets of Cairo," showing
the Egyptians in native costume, with their camels bedecked
and ready to take you for a ride. Some of these people are
educated, and some can talk a little English, while all seem to

know what money is, and look for compensation for everything that they do for you, even to posing for their pictures.

Then you can enter the city of "Jerusalem" through a
gate. This city is surrounded by a reproduction of the
original walls of that ancient city, and the interior is built as
was ancient Jerusalem, with the "Jaffa" gate, and the narrow streets and the old places of abode which these people
occupied. Jerusalem is not on "The Pike," but off by itself
in the grounds of the "Fair." There are little shop windows,
or booths, on the sides of the streets where you can purchase
souvenirs of their handiwork.

The "Filipino Village" is an interesting place to visit,
especially at the time of the "drills," when these courteous
little dark-complexioned Filipinos perform a perfect and
interesting drill, marching to the music of the band, composed of Filipinos who play upon American brass horns
and instruments of music, directed by one of our American
band masters, all attired in the United States army dress.
We cannot but admire the willing, progressive boys who,
in three years of kindness and education by our great
United States, have proved suitable and faithful bearers of
the glorious "Star-Spangled Banner," which they certainly feel proud to wave over their heads. This shows what
education and civilization can do in three years. Of course
the savage tribes called the "Igorotes" have not, as yet, been
conquered, but there is a space allotted for these people.
The "Igorotes" remind one of fine bronze statues, as their
skin is polished and shaded so that they are really artistic
from that point of view, with the exception of their faces.
They wear no clothes—only a girdle—and it is said that they
live on dog meat; but I trust now, that as we have them in
this country, they will soon become a little more civilized.
Their music is of the kind that makes you wish that you
were deaf, and you are ready to pay them to stop. It sounds
very much like that made by little white Indians when they

are pounding on dishpans and all sorts of noisy things. These people live in bungalows with a kind of straw for the roof, and many of these buildings are now erected in the Filipino village.

I trust that the "Humane Society" will prevent them from using dog meat in our country, for it is sad to think that man's most faithful friend is slaughtered for food by savages. There are a great many things to see on the "Pike," for there are amusements of all kinds to catch the pennies. Real live Indians, too, can be seen daily on dress parade.

There is an Indian village on the Fair Grounds, and one can see the Indians living in wigwams, or tepees, and cooking their meals out of doors upon stoves made of stones.

"The Pike" is the place to have fun, but the main "Fair," with the beautiful buildings and magnificent architecture, with the lovely rolling grounds of its park, is a sight that I wish all children could see.

The Indian school is a credit to our country, as it shows what we have done to better the Indians, some of whom seem willing to learn, and to live more like the white man. There are plenty of little pappooses, and they enjoy being carried around on their mother's backs. Occasionally, however, one sees a squaw carrying her pappoose on her arm, as a white mother does, and this looks strangely out of place.

CHAPTER XXVIII

BEAUTIFUL JIM KEY

VALUED AT ONE MILLION DOLLARS

It gives me great pleasure to introduce to my little readers, particularly those who have not been so fortunate as to make his acquaintance, this remarkable horse, "Jim Key," who is counted among the wonders of these days of progress and education. I consider it a great privilege to tell the history of this famous horse, and to use his photograph, presented to me by his present owner, Mr. A. R. Rogers, of New York City. Beautiful Jim Key is now thirteen years old, and is of a handsome mahogany-bay color, of the Arabian type, with a long black tail and mane. He has a thoughtful and knowing expression in his black eyes which speaks the kindness that he expresses by his belonging to the "Jim Key Band of Mercy." This Band tries to benefit all animals, and surely "Jim Key" was sent here to help all his four-footed friends. You, little children, who read this, can each belong to this Band of Mercy if you will send your name to Mr. A. R. Rogers, 75 Maiden Lane, New York City, who is president of this band, or to Mr. George T. Angell, president of "The American Humane Education Society," No. 19 Milk Street, Boston, Mass. The pledge to this Band is, "I will try to be kind to all harmless living creatures, and try to protect them from cruel usages." If you will send your name on a slip of paper with this pledge written on it, with your address, it will be pasted on the great banner roll of "Jim Key Band of Mercy." Thousands of adults, as well as 300,000 children, belong to this band now. The humane paper called "Our Dumb Animals," is a splendid

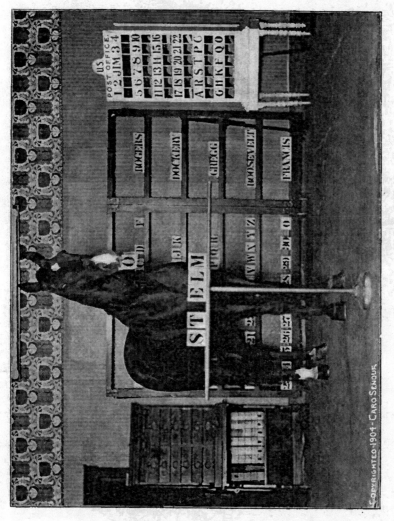

BEAUTIFUL JIM KEY
SPELLING "ST. ELMO" AT THE "WORLD'S FAIR," ST. LOUIS

journal for lovers of animals, and is but twenty-five cents a year. It is certainly helping a worthy cause. We all wish to do some good in this world, and by aiding the helpless animals we are surely doing a work of charity, as they cannot tell their troubles to us. In consequence, they are obliged to stand the hardships of life unless some kind person lends a helping hand. Beautiful Jim Key was born in Ten-

nessee, and was faithfully cared for by his old master, Dr. William Key, who, although nearly seventy years old, still exhibits him. These two have been constant companions, and it is a touching sight to see the love between this good, kind gentleman and his trusting horse. "Jim" showed unusual traits from the time that he was a colt, for he would follow his master around as a dog will do, and he was so curious to see and to know what everything was that he soon learned how to do many things. One of the first things that he learned, and he taught this to himself, was to unfasten the gate and let himself out in the road. His master began to teach him when he was one year old. To me he is a marvel of intellect, and I shall try to tell you, as accurately as possible, about his knowledge of school.

First. Jim opens school, that is, he rings the bell for school to open. Jim goes to his little trunk and pushes up the cover with his nose, takes out two bells by the handles, and holding them tightly in his mouth, he shakes them while walking around the stage, and so he rings his class to order.

Second. Jim picks out any letter of the alphabet, playing-card, or number asked for. On a tall rack behind him are alphabetically arranged all the letters on white paste-board cards, about the size of a playing card, with each letter printed in large black type; and when any one in the audience asks him for a letter, he walks to this rack and with his mouth gently takes the one asked for, and brings it right side up to the front of the stage. He likes applause; so one must always remember that and give him plenty of hand-clapping, as he deserves more than any two hands can give him.

Third. Jim shows his proficiency in figuring, adding, multiplying, dividing, and subtracting in any numbers below thirty. This is really the most marvelous test of horse intellect that I ever have seen performed. The numbers are arranged on a rack in a similar way to the letters, beginning with No. 1, and all the numbers are in large, black type so they can be seen in the back of the room. You can give him any example you wish, using numbers that will not bring your answer above thirty, and he will surprise you by bringing to the front of the platform in his mouth the card on which is your answer, sometimes before you can ascertain it yourself. And he knows in a second that you cannot subtract a larger number from a smaller one, for he always shakes his head to signify that it cannot be done. I myself asked him to subtract four from three, and in an instant his head was shaking "No." Again, I asked him to bring this answer, "two plus three, multiply by six," and he brought out the number for the answer, thirty; and again, I said, "two plus three plus five plus eight," and he returned to the front with eighteen. And one example, which a man gave him, had to be put down on paper before I could get the answer. Jim had it first, and it was this, and I am sure that any of you thirteen-year-old children will be obliged either to put the numbers down, or to go over them more than once. Just think of a horse's figuring out this example: "Three times ten, divided by two, plus five, divided by two, minus ten," and the fine calculator came to the front with zero card for his answer. Was he correct? I attended three different days, and no two questions were given him the same, so I feel convinced that this wonderful horse has intellect which is beyond animals.

Fourth. Jim spells any ordinary name asked him. A long spindle, having a thin nickel rail with a slit along the top, is placed in the front of the platform, and names were given him to spell, such as chair, James, Carrie, and a hard name, "Carey," which was a little boy's name. When I heard the child sing out "Carey," I myself wondered whether it was spelt with an "e" or whether it was "Cary"; but Jim knew at once, and went to the rack and brought each letter forward, one at a time, until he had the five letters. Then he stood still for the little boy to tell him whether he was correct, and he was; and you well know that it is not a common name. I was really surprised and delighted.

Fifth. He reads and writes.

Sixth. Jim goes to the postoffice, gets the mail from any box requested, and files the letter in a regular letter-file under any letter asked him. This is a wonderful piece of calculation also. A letter section is arranged with numbers on, and letters of the alphabet are on the lower edges of each pigeon-hole which contains mail. When you ask him to get your mail from "M" box, he takes the letter with his mouth out of the place, and walks across the stage and lays the letter upon the shelf of his desk or letter-file, and waits until he is told where to file it; then he pulls out the drawer and takes up the letter, drops it in the drawer and closes it, and after he has answered as many of these requests as you wish, he pulls down the outside cover of the tier of files, which closes up his desk for that performance.

Seventh.   Jim distinguishes various pieces of money, and goes to a cash register and rings up any amount asked for, bringing the correct change.   Now, this is another mark of his great knowledge.   If you ask him to get a dollar bill, he goes to the register, pulls open the drawer, and takes out the dollar bill, or he will bring a silver dollar, a half-dollar, quarter, or even a nickel out of his register, and when he comes to the front of the stage he holds the money between his handsome teeth, and grins so that you can see the money; and his master will say, "Grin, Jim," and Jim really grins.

Eighth.   Gives quotations from the Bible, where the horse is mentioned, giving chapter and verse.   This he does by choosing from his assortment of names on the racks the exact one which corresponds with the Bible.

Tenth.   Uses the telephone.   The telephone is on the wall, and he walks up to it, takes the handle in his mouth, and turns the handle around so that you can hear the bell ring, then he places his mouth to the mouth-piece, and his master takes the receiver and holds it to his ear.   When his master says "good-by" Jim goes back to his place, always facing the audience.

Eleventh.   Jim takes a silver dollar from the bottom of a glass jar filled with water, without drinking a drop.   (Considered one of the greatest feats ever performed by an animal.)   This glass jar holds about five gallons of water, and you can see Jim through the glass picking up the silver dollar, never sipping a drop.   When he holds it up to you and grins, his face is wet and the water drips down, so he goes to his little trunk, lifts up the lid with his nose, and takes out a fringed towel, which he gives to his master for him to wipe his face, after which he returns the towel to his trunk, and tucks in all the fringe. He has so many friends among the ladies and children that sugar and towels and apples are sent him as presents, and one lady sent him some fringed towels tied together with ribbons and embroidered with his name in one corner. Jim is very fond of sugar in the little cubes, and after each answer he receives a piece, for which he is always ready, looking sidewise for his reward. I could tell you some other lessons, but I think when dear Jim does all these that he is busy enough. I hope that after the little readers have become acquainted with this wonderful horse, they will think of him always, and help all poor animals who are in need of homes and kind treatment, and above all report all cases which they may see of abuse of horses, either by whipping them or by making them draw overloaded wagons. And try to keep water in your yards for the dogs, cats, and birds, and do what you can to have watering-places for horses in the streets. All this will help "Beautiful Jim Key" in his work of befriending animals, and please remember that this educated horse was taught by *kindness*. There is a little book of his life and how he was taught, which one can buy for fifteen cents by sending to Mr. A. R. Rogers, 75 Maiden Lane, New York City.

Long live "Beautiful Jim Key."

                                        CARO SENOUR.

CHAPTER XXIX

Now, I am going to talk again, for my mistress, like all the ladies, never knows when to stop talking, and when she gets started on the animal question some one has to say "mouse." Well, my family says if my mistress had remained at the "World's Fair" much longer, she would either have eloped with "Beautiful Jim Key" or have joined his performances, as she said she would go to see him every day, and would spend all her money on his exhibitions, for she always learned something from him. She went up to him and put her arms around his neck and kissed him five times, and Jim seemed to like it. He is as glossy as a piece of satin, and I do not feel a bit jealous because my mistress admires him so much. He is a noble horse, and I, with my mistress, love and respect "Beautiful Jim Key."

Now that my mistress has told you her side of the great World's Fair Exposition, I shall give you the funny side of it, which always interests me, as I am a good fellow to see a joke. I wondered why my mistress and my cousin "Bert" kept the "Pike" visit for the last, but after I had been on the "Pike" for five minutes I understood, for, after you once land there, it is almost impossible to get away, as there are so very many curious people and things to see.

The music of the "Streets of Cairo" was maddening to most people, but I enjoyed it so much that I went right up to the funny drum and wanted to investigate it, which made the men of Egypt laugh while they tried to blow their horns, and the louder the noise the more fun I had. The man at the door invited me in, and I was about to accept his invitation when I peeped through the big gateway and saw a mountain raising itself out of the ground, which made me look up

148

so high that it tired my neck; so I backed out, and after two or
three of these four-footed mountains with sharp peaks arose,
I saw that each one had four feet, one long neck, and a
wiggling head. Then the man said, "Come and ride the
camel," and I finally grasped the idea, and felt ashamed
that I had not recognized one of my four-footed "nationalities." We thanked him and passed on. We took a picture
of the big seven-foot Arab on his camel; and the camel was
like me, it being so long that its head could not get on the
plate, so I am sorry not to be able to show you the picture,
but he did have a head. But my! if I just had *its* long neck,
couldn't I see everything? You see, we are different, that
is, a camel has a long neck and short tail, and I have a long
tail and short neck, so it is not evenly divided. I was sorry
that "Dan" was not with me, but inasmuch as the "Fair" is
closed to dogs, he has been able only to peek through the
high fence and has missed lots of fun. Just think, poor
"Klondyke" can't see the "Pike" either, and it is a great
neglect in one's education not to "do the Pike."

The next funny thing that we witnessed was performed
by a real live Indian, dressed up in blankets, feathers, and
all color complexion washes. He certainly had just been
to a "beauty parlor." Well, he was a picture, and I was
thankful that he was not my master. He was a monster,
and when I first gazed upon him he was bending over a
letter-box, holding a letter in his right hand and his blanket
tightly grasped in his left hand. He was looking for the
place in which to put the letter, and it was a sight to see his
frozen face change when my cousin "Bert" opened the lift for
him and showed him how to post his letter. But the "smile
that won't come off" was certainly fastened to his face, and
I feared that I had lost my dear cousin "Bert," for the Indian
seemed perfectly fascinated with her, and her ability to open
that letter-box.

After this we went again to see "Beautiful Jim Key,"

and I was "passed in" there and invited to take a front seat, and see the wonderful horse.   I sat on a chair, and was very much interested in his school training, but I think, to tell the truth, that I was more interested in the sugar that was given him after each answer.   I did lie down on the floor a while when he was doing the fine spelling, which is beyond my education, but the ringing of the bells and the telephoning, also the fishing in the glass jar for the silver dollar and the wiping of his face with a fringed towel, then putting the towel away in his little trunk, all this really puzzled me, and I remained quiet all through the entertainment.   I want to tell you here that during all those six hours at "The Fair" I never barked or growled once, but there were many things which I was anxious to express my feelings about, but I remembered my lecture in the morning before coming, and I wanted to be invited again, so I was good.   I was a little bit afraid of a peculiar looking man who stood in front of this place and attracted the crowds, for he was dressed in loose white and red humpty-dumpty clothes with a tiny hat on one side of his head.   He made me shake until I found out he was just in play, and that his business name was "Clown."

I think that I enjoyed the ride around the grounds on the "Intramural" electric railroad about the best, for I saw all the buildings and the grounds, and I had a whole seat to myself and a large open window to look through, so that was solid comfort.   The Indians were preparing their supper out of doors, and the pappooses were strapped to their mothers' backs, and some, large enough to walk around, were playing, and were not overburdened with clothes.   I saw one little fellow run up and knock his friend down with his fist, and the "downed" fellow returned the compliment by picking up his mother's wooden ladle and gently landing it upon his companion's head.   His mother rushed out and picked up her ladle from the dirt, spanked her darling with it, then placed it in the kettle to dish out the soup. It is convenient for the mothers to be able to use one utensil for all the necessities of the camp, and as they have no slippers, as our mamas have, a spoon is *very* handy.

The little savage Filipinos are rather fascinating little children to watch. They are dark in color, with black woolly (I should say naturally curly) hair, standing up bushy all around their little black faces. My mistress tried for fifteen minutes to get a snap-shot at them, but the cunning little chaps would hide as soon as she would lift the kodak, and peep out from around the corner of their bungalows.

Another good exhibition on the "Pike" is the "trained animals" exhibit. These animals are all wonderfully trained, such as the seals, lions, tigers, and other wild animals. The seals really perform extraordinary feats. They play on brass instruments, such as cymbals, and beat the drums, and balance balls upon their noses, and do many clever tricks, and they seem very willing to perform.

The wild animals in the cages do fine tricks. This is just the place for children to enjoy themselves.

I could tell you many other good things at this exhibition, but time and space prevent. However, I must say in closing this chapter that my family thinks the "World's Fair" at St. Louis a great success, and a beautiful picture never to be forgotten. For myself I thank all the kind people of that hospitable city who added so greatly to my happiness and who have contributed so much interesting matter for my book. I wish this great exposition every possible success, and I say, "Long live dear, old St. Louis."

CHAPTER XXX

I suppose you boys have wondered whether I have a "pedigree." Well, I have a pedigree, and one that I am very proud of, and that pedigree is the honor of being born in the United States of America; and that is a pedigree worthy to possess. Well! I have a "dog-pedigree" in the "Lone Star" state, and we could get it of course, but my mistress says that I am not a "dog-show-dog," and that I require no outline as to my ancestors for I am her pet and not her "show-dog," and what I do to please the children I do for love. My mistress also says that my ancestors were of course English, but that all my ancestral country is lost track of in my American democratic life and ways. I am an American, and that is all any true American need say.

I hope you will not think it egotistical in me to say so here, but my mistress told some friends the other day that after all the courtesies and honors shown St. Elmo, he is the same sweet, kind dog to the poor forlorn dogs and children as he was when a little Kansas "bow-wow." I merely tell you this to say that whatever our advantages are over others we should always remember to be natural, never to show our superior position, and in this way we shall be loved and shall make others happy.

I thank my little readers for their kind attention, and sincerely hope that I have made some sweet little child happy by giving to him or to her the true happenings of my short life, and if I have done any good by writing this book in behalf of my animal kingdom, my mission will have been fulfilled; and once more I wish to ask you all to remember my motto, then I shall say good-by to my dear little friends.

"By being kind to all animals, and by protecting horses and dogs, you are befriending man's best and most faithful friends."

Trustingly yours,

ST. ELMO.

My Playthings

LaVergne, TN USA
13 December 2009
166843LV00004B/111/A